CELEBRATING LIFE

LAWS, LIES, POWERS & TRUTHS OF THE

UNIVERSE

JIM JOHNSON

First published by Dog Ear Publishing
4010 W. 86th Street, Ste H
Indianapolis, IN 46268
www.dogearpublishing.net

ISBN: 978-1-4575-1518-7

This book is printed on acid-free paper.

Printed in the United States of America

ABOUT THE AUTHOR

JIM JOHNSON is a recovering Southern Baptist, a student of Unity, a student of Spiritualism, an ordained minister in A Course In Miracles, and a Certified Hypnotherapist. Scholastically, he has a BS in Chemical Engineering, and an MBA. He spent most of his career as a Naval Officer an Army Education Officer, a University Math Professor, and a Real Estate Investor.

With his varied background, Jim has put his analytical mind to work in writing books that reveal his interest and concern for his fellow planet-dwellers. His previous book, ***SUCCESS THROUGH SELF-HYPNOSIS*** dealt with his hypnotherapy training. Jim has written scripts and published a seven CD Self-Hypnosis album, ***HYPNODYNAMIX,*** covering 21 behavior modification topics.

His previous book, ***WELCOME TO THE STATE OF JOY***, embraces four life-changing teachings into one program, teaching the reader how to achieve peace of mind and live in a state of joy.

Jim is a sought-after speaker delivering the message, Change Your Thinking...Change Your Life. If you change the way you think, you will change the way you act, and you will change the way that people respond to you. When not writing or speaking, Jim is a performing tap dancer... celebrating life.

NOTE FROM THE AUTHOR

Like a ship without a compass, most of us sail through life with no idea of where we're going. The problem is that most of us don't know what it is we actually want. We end up sailing from one destination to the next, hoping to find what we're seeking through luck rather than through purpose.

CELEBRATING LIFE offers an alternative to this hit-miss approach. It explains how to create a happier and more purposeful life by providing a compass causing you to navigate your journey on the Physical Plane. Learning and practicing the material presented in this book is a means of achieving your full potential. This process is a symbol of self- worth, of caring about you, activating your Power Within.

Before your soul incarnated onto the Physical Plane to experience the journey on which you have embarked, your soul dwelled on the Astral Plane. When your soul makes its transition from the Physical Plane, it will return to the Astral Plane. The purpose of ***CELEBRATING LIFE*** is to assist you to live the life your soul intended while you are incarnated on the Physical Plane during this incarnation.

CELEBRATING LIFE is a reminder of life's everyday magic, of how powerful you are, and of how far you can reach and achieve. Sometimes it's easy to lose sight of these truths particularly living on a Physical Plane that insists that we're limited, aging creatures, stuck somewhere between luck and fate. A life properly lived is an easy, luxurious life. It's not supposed to be hard, though we can make it that way with wrong-minded thinking, low expectations, or failing to see ourselves as we really are… loving son's of God… infinite beings of light. We are fun-loving gladiators of the Universe, adventurers just being human, with eternity before us and the power of our thoughts to shape it.

We are going to deal with some powerful material. You will learn how to turn yourself loose in ways you have never been turned loose before. You will discard some obsolete beliefs which will give you new insights. You will learn to achieve goals you never thought were possible before… personal goals, financial goals, spiritual goals, and career goals. There is no limit to your achievement potential. You will learn the art of ***CELEBRATING LIFE.***

CELEBRATING LIFE can also be used as an effective resource for inspirational speakers. Each of the topics could easily be material for a 10-15 minute inspirational talk.

TABLE OF CONTENTS

CHAPTER ONE
LAWS OF THE UNIVERSE

The laws of the Universe are laws of metaphysics.
Webster's New Collegiate Dictionary
offers the following definitions:

METAPHYSICS: The branch of **philosophy** which deals with first principles and seeks to explain the nature of being and the origin and structure of the Universe… the **science** of universal order.

PHILOSOPHY: A study of the processes governing **thought**… investigation of the principles that regulate the **Universe** and underlie all reality.

SCIENCE: Knowledge of facts or principles gained by a systematic study, dealing with a body of **truths** systematically arranged and showing the operation of general laws.

The key words in these definitions are:

THOUGHT, ORDER, TRUTHS, LAWS, UNIVERSE

These laws of truth and order are in effect at all times. We are using these laws whether or not we are aware of our doing so. The name of the game is to use them to our advantage.

THE LAW OF ATTRACTION

THE LAW OF CHANGE

THE LAW OF INCREASE

THE LAW OF VISION

THE LAW OF GROWTH

THE LAW OF ATTRACTION

Like attracts like.
Like begets like.
Thoughts become things.

You have three states of mind… your Conscious Mind, your Sub-Conscious Mind, and your Cosmic Mind. All of your thoughts come from your Conscious Mind, and every one of your thoughts vibrates at a positive vibration or it vibrates at a negative vibration.

All of the truth in your Cosmic Mind is vibrating at a positive vibration. Your Cosmic Mind has always been with you. It is Your Spiritual DNA. It is called by many names: Father Within, Christ Consciousness, Higher-Self, I AM, Divine Source, Divine Mind, Divine Power, Divine Love, Holy Spirit, Intuition, God. This is where inspiration comes from. It is all-knowing.

You say… "How do I get in touch with my Cosmic Mind?" You don't have to get in touch with it. All you have to do is to acknowledge its presence. When you ask for Guidance, your Cosmic Mind will send you a hunch, an intuitive hint. You know how that goes. It is the way your Cosmic Mind communicates with you.

Some religious people get nervous when we say that God resides within us. The entire presence of God is everywhere, at all times. Your Cosmic Mind is the perfection within you, your sense of well-being, your peace of mind, your Highest and Best.

Every time you send out a thought from your Conscious Mind, its vibration is checked out by your Cosmic Mind.

If the vibrations are alike, you experience a right-minded emotion:

Joy
Disappointment
Empowerment
Love
Appreciation
Passion.
Enthusiasm
Positive Expectation
Optimism
Hopefulness
Contentment

If the vibrations are not alike, you experience a wrong-minded emotion:

Boredom
Doubt
Worry
Blame
Discouragement
Pessimism
Frustration
Irritation
Impatience
Overwhelm
Anger
Rage
Revenge
Hatred
Jealousy
Insecurity
Guilt
Unworthiness
Fear
Grief
Depression
Despair
Powerlessness

You know if your Conscious Mind thinking is aligned with your Cosmic Mind if you are feeling good. A bad feeling is an indicator that your Conscious Mind thinking is not in alignment with your Cosmic Mind.

Suppose your Conscious Mind sends out the negative thought... I never have enough money. The positive truth in your Cosmic Mind says... You are entitled to be prosperous. It is your birthright. The vibration mismatch causes you to feel a bad emotion, which is an indicator that your Conscious Mind thinking is not in alignment with your Cosmic Mind. On the other hand, suppose your Conscious Mind sends out the positive thought... I am grateful for my prosperity. The vibration match causes you to feel good. It behooves you to feel good because the consequences of feeling bad... a feeling of dis-ease... can cause depression, despair and disease.

Not only that... every time you send out a thought from your Conscious Mind, it not only must pass muster with your Cosmic Mind, it is also projected out into the Universe, where it finds its like vibration. So… when your Conscious Mind sends out the negative thought… I never have enough money… it finds its like vibration in the Universe, and never having enough money is manifested and becomes your reality.

Like attracts like.

Every thought that has ever been thought or ever will be thought is lurking out in the Universe, just waiting for a thought from your Conscious Mind to vibrate at its frequency so that it can latch onto it and manifest into your reality. When you send out thoughts of lack, depression, despair, anger, those are the situations that manifest into your reality. When you send out thoughts of love, happiness, prosperity, joy, those are the situations that manifest into your reality. You are a powerful person. You have the power to create your reality. Actually… you do create your reality, like it or not. The Law of Attraction is always at work. The name of the game is to make it work to your advantage. You can have anything you want. If you can think it, you can have it. The problem is… most people attract what they don't want. How many times have you heard someone say… "I am always stressed out…My relationships always end in disaster… Money just seems to elude me…I am not a healthy person." These negative thoughts find their vibrational match, and the Universe responds accordingly, and with abundance.

Like begets like.

The purpose of your being in your physical body on the planet in time and space is to experience the joy of the trip… to feel good. When you take a vacation, you leave home, you stay for a certain amount of time, and you come back home. Then you say… WOW… that was a great trip. Well… why else would you have left home?

When you left Home and decided to take the trip you are now experiencing in your physical body, during this particular incarnation, you did not plan to have a bummer trip. The way you can always feel good is for your thoughts from your Conscious Mind to be a vibrational match with the truth in your Cosmic Mind. That's how you manage to feel good. The way you experience prosperity, perfect health, and healthy relationships is for your Conscious Mind to project those thoughts out into the Universe so that those situations can manifest into your reality.

To illustrate how you can manifest what you want, **on purpose**, I have a story for you. In May 2008, I took a cruise with Mike Dooley around the Hawaiian Islands. Mike Dooley writes a daily e-mail column entitled *Notes From The Universe*. His web site is: www.tut.com. There were 40 of us who were TUT devotees.

During the 7-day cruise, Mike gave 5 workshops entitled *Manifesting Your Reality*. He urged us to visualize 15 minutes every day, when we got home. He said not to exceed that time limit or we would get tired of it and not do it any more. During this 15-minute process, we were to visualize something that we desired… not bothering to consider *how* it was to manifest. He said the cursed how's were the job of the Universe.

So… if you are at point A and you want to be at point B… visualize yourself already there. Express gratitude for already being there. Act as if you are already there. Feel the good feeling of being there. Pretend you are there. Fake it 'till you make it.

Well… when I got home, I decided to give it a GO. I decided to visualize that my $450,000.00 mortgage on my house was paid off, and that money was pouring in. There was no way I could imagine *how* that could happen. However… I could imagine its happening. I visualized a big piece of paper that had MORTGAGE written on it. I saw it going up in flames… going… going… gone. I visualized a big cast iron pot with gold coins pouring into it. I did this for 15 minutes, each day for 3 months. One morning, the phone rang and a lady's voice said: "Is this Jim Johnson?" I responded affirmatively. She said: "Mr. John- son, we want to pay off your mortgage, and give you $250,000.00." I said: "Well… it's about time." (After all… I had been visualizing faithfully for 3 months.) She continued to explain that she represented a Reverse Mortgage company, that they had appraised my house, and based on an appraisal value of $1.5 million, and my age of 73, that is how they made their determination. She further explained that the first step in the process was for their appraiser to come and actually appraise the house. The appraiser came 2 days later. The house did not appraise at the estimated value. However… it appraised high enough for the mortgage to be paid off and there was money left over.

Now… I had never heard of a Reverse Mortgage company. I had no idea *how* my visualized desire could possibly become my manifested reality. The point is… when your positive thought vibrates at the frequency of its counterpart in the Universe, the Universe will arrange people, places and events to cause it to manifest into your reality.

So... whatever you want, hoping, wishing, begging will not get it for you. Here's how to get it!

**AN END RESULT
VISUALIZED WITH EXPECTATION
WILL ALWAYS FORCE THE CIRCUMSTANCES
NECESSARY TO CAUSE ITS MANIFESTATION,
NO MATTER HOW UNLIKELY OR EVEN IMPOSSIBLE
THOSE CIRCUMSTANCES MAY HAVE PREVIOUSLY SEEMED.**

So... how do you visualize an end result with expectation? Here are the 8 exciting steps that activate the manifesting power:

1. SEE THE END RESULT AS IF IT HAS ALREADY HAPPENED. THIS IS FUTURE SPEAKING TO YOURSELF.
2. THOUGHTS BECOME THINGS.
3. DO IT EVERY DAY. THOUGHTS HELD IN MIND PRODUCE AFTER THEIR OWN KIND.
4. DO IT FOR 5 MINUTES. THIS IS TIME ENOUGH.
5. SEE EVERY DETAIL. IT'S YOUR STORY.
6. PUT YOURSELF IN THE PICTURE. YOU ARE THE STAR.
7. EXPRESS GRATITUDE IN ADVANCE.
8. THE UNIVERSE RESPONDS TO GRATITUDE WITH ABUNDANCE.
9. DON'T MESS WITH THE CURSED "HOWS". THAT'S NOT YOUR JOB.
10. THAT'S THE JOB OF THE UNIVERSE.
11. BEHAVE AS IF IT HAS ALREADY HAPPENED. FAKE IT 'TILL YOU MAKE IT.

Thoughts become things.

It should now be obvious that it would be to your advantage for your Conscious Mind to automatically send out thoughts that have positive vibrations for 2 reasons:

So that there is a vibrational match with your Cosmic Mind, causes you to feel good. So that the positive vibration will find its positive match in the Universe, causing positive events to manifest into your reality.

How can you ensure that your Conscious Mind is sending out positive vibrations, automatically?

That's where the Sub-Conscious Mind comes in. The Sub-Conscious Mind does not think, analyze, or act. It is the autopilot for the Conscious Mind. The Sub-Conscious Mind is where all your habit patterns are stored. If you have a habit, behavior, or thought pattern that you would like to change, all you have to do is to re-program your Sub-Conscious Mind. Since it does not think or analyze, it will believe anything you tell it. Your new, desired thought is your new way of thinking, automatically. It's as simple as that.

The question is… how do I re-program my Sub-Conscious Mind to provide automatic, positive thoughts to my Conscious Mind? The process is to get your Conscious Mind out of the way so that you can direct positive thoughts directly to your Sub-Conscious Mind… the mind that believes anything you tell it.

The question is… how do I do that?
The answer is… Self-Hypnosis.

So… here you are, a spiritual being, a loving child of God, on a joyous trip, living in a physical body, living in time and space on the planet, thinking positive thoughts that match the vibration of the truth in your Cosmic Mind causing you to feel good, thinking positive thoughts that match the positive vibration in the Universe causing the Universe to manifest your desires into your reality.

WOW… you are a powerful person.

CONGRATULATIONS!

You are using the Law of Attraction to your advantage.

SELF-HYPNOSIS

Giving the Conscious Mind powerful, positive suggestions is important and constructive. However... giving these same suggestions to your Sub-Conscious Mind is 10 times more powerful. At the conscious level, we try to make changes in our lives. At the Sub-Conscious level, we make changes in our lives. It is not enough to convince your Conscious Mind that changing habits is possible. Only as you learn to reprogram your Sub-Conscious Mind, will you be able to satisfy the Conscious Mind desires. The Sub-Conscious desires always over-ride the conscious desires. The Sub-Conscious Mind is the auto-pilot to the Conscious Mind. The Conscious Mind can over-ride the auto-pilot temporarily by accepting a positive suggestion, but in an instant... whatever was already programmed in the auto-pilot will take over. Permanent change can occur only by reprogramming the auto-pilot. We always do what our Sub-Conscious Mind believes.

Now that you are convinced that communicating with the Sub-Conscious Mind is the key to changing behavior patterns, the question than arises: How do I communicate with my Sub-Conscious Mind? The answer is learning and practicing Self-Hypnosis.

The hypnotic state is an altered state of consciousness whether it is induced by a facilitator or whether it is self-induced. This relaxed state is similar to that of Meditation and Prayer. During this altered, relaxed state, the Conscious Mind is set aside allowing the positive, powerful suggestions to be transmitted directly to the Sub-Conscious Mind which is non-critical and believes everything it hears.

The question now arises:

How does one do Self-Hypnosis?

There are 3 steps involved in the Self-Hypnosis exercise:

Induction... achieving the altered, relaxed state of consciousness by suggesting relaxation.

Message... making the positive, powerful re-programming suggestions to the fully forward Sub-Conscious Mind.

Arousal... suggestions used to bring you back to the conscious state.

The most effective way of experiencing Self-Hypnosis is to listen to a CD... either one you have made, or one you have purchased. Otherwise, a facilitator will be required.

t and then you know what they are not going to work out. Faith works

t is that you have faith in that's what you bring about. If you have faith not going to succeed or that this is never going to work for you, of oesn't, because your faith is bringing that about. If you have faith that it if you have faith that life can get better, that things will happen, well of will.

Choice

cond aspect of this law of change is choice. People think they have no ey don't realize that every decision they make is a choice. Every y, every challenge that we experience confronts us with a choice. We ose a positive approach or we choose a negative approach. Even if we firmative choice at all we do approach a mind set when we move into

us to change our life for the better, we must affirmatively identify with a nd what that better life means to us. It's easy to say I want a better life ou thought about what a better life looks like to you?

ecide what you want in your life and then you begin to focus on that. Now on how that's going to happen, just focus on the end result. See yourself e result of that choice. In other words, if you are choosing a success in a ter, see yourself living out that success and then the Universe will work out bring it to you. It will work out the absolutely perfect avenue for that to u and I think that we have to choose how things are going to happen to us ot the truth. The Universe has enough intelligence to work that out on its st live in end result.

Desire

spect of the law of change is desire. The key ingredient for change is burning desire. Unless you have a really deep hunger, a burning desire then it probably won't happen. I'm going to tell you that I quit smoking nes, I was good at quitting, but then I would start back again because I a burning desire to quit. I quit for all the wrong reasons. I quit because ted me to quit, I quit because I thought I should quit, I quit for all those d then I went back to smoking. I couldn't really quit.

ecided not that I shouldn't or it wasn't good for me. I decided I didn't want nymore. I really didn't want to smoke anymore. I decided I don't want to oke in my lungs. This is crazy. The minute I made that decision, I never had arette. I never even wanted another cigarette. But you see I had a desire to

SELF-HYPNOSIS SCRIPT

THE INDUCTION

Make your body very comfortable. Relax. Close out everything from the outside world. Get a sense of inner quiet, peace, harmony into your being as you focus your eyes on any spot in a wide-open stare. Keep staring at that spot. You will find your eyes quickly get- ting tired. The lids get heavier and heavier. And now… close your eyes. Roll the eyeballs backwards. Take a deep breath. Let the eyes relax. Let the jaw relax. Let the shoulders go down. As your breath goes down slowly, everything goes intorelaxation.

Now… imagine you have weights on your eyelids, making them feel so heavy and relaxed. Go deeper and deeper into this marvelous relaxed state. Your Sub-Conscious Mind is now fully forward… ready to accept positive, powerful suggestions.

THE MESSAGE

I like and respect myself, and others.

I know that I am a worthy and capable person. I look for ways to put myself and others up.

I show concern for the feelings of others. I write realistic, achievable goals.

All of my body systems are working in harmony to keep me healthy. I enjoy taking calculated risks to improve.

I call on HOLY SPIRIT for Guidance at all times. I am ever vigilant against the EGO thought system. I am grateful for my abundance.

I extend Love to all Loving Children of God. I enjoy sharing my abundance.

I write positive, goal-achieving affirmations each day with delight and enjoyment.

I am God's Son, complete and healed and whole, shining in the reflection of His Love. In me is His creation sanctified and guaranteed eternal life.

In me is love perfected, fear impossible, and joy established without opposite. I am the holy home of God Himself.

I am the Heaven where His Love resides.

I am His Holy Sinlessness Itself, for in my purity abides his Own.

THE AROUSAL

At each daily Self-Hypnosis practice, you will tell yourself: Next time, I will go deeper. And now… count from 5 to 1 for arousal. 5… remembering all that you need to remember. 4… take your suggestions deep within. Your Sub-Conscious Mind has locked them in… deeply embedded. 3… the blood begins to surge through your veins from the tip of your toes to the top of your head. All the organs are working in perfect harmony… perfect coordination. 2… coming up, feeling fine, coming alert, feeling wonderful. And… 1… wide awake, feeling great and full of energy… feeling fine

MAKING SELF-HYPNOSIS WORK

You now know that learning and practicing Self-Hypnosis is a natural and effective way to gain access to your Sub-Conscious Mind. It is a means of achieving your full potential.

When you are in the hypnotic state of consciousness, the Conscious Mind is not working and you can program any goal you wish into your Sub-Conscious Mind. You can use Self-Hypnosis to make your life more joyful, smoother, and better in every respect. The breaking of an addictive habit, or the accomplishing of any objective is a tremendous achievement. As a result of your accomplishment, you will find an upsurge of new confidence in your own inner being that will carry over into everything you do in life.

THE LAW OF CHA

Faith
Choice
Desire

We've all heard that there is nothing sure in life e
changing and you and I can probably agree on
experienced in life is when we've stayed too long w
should leave. I look back on my life and every time I
too long at the fair. Some- thing happens and it's wo
and we say this is it. And then because life is chan
And then we begin to have pain in our life because w

We haven't learned that life does evolve and what wa
not necessarily right now. One of the laws for succes
2:12 says... *And be not conformed to this world but y*
of your mind. Isn't that telling you change your mi
conformed to this world means that you're not locke
or situations or associations or challenges that exist
not locked into that. You do not have to remain in t
be transformed by the renewing of your mind. In ot
is to change your mind and then of course you chang

What we think, we create. In other words you can c
it is right now to anything you want it to be by chang

The law of change has 3 fundame

Faith

First of all we have to have faith in the law. Faith is d
in something or someone generally before there's an
from which all doubt is removed, that's the difference
have a biblical definition of faith which makes it reall
that comes from is Hebrews 11:1. *Now faith is the s*
the evidence of things not seen. What this means is t
change in your life you must have faith that it's p
negative any situation is that we're in, how absolutel
to be, if you have faith that things will get better th
Faith is that first step toward finding it. And if you
change then you have faith in those doubts, you have

to work o
both ways

Whatever
that you'
course it
will work
course th

Now the s
choice. T
opportuni
either ch
have no a
somethin

In order f
better life
but have y

You must
don't focu
living in t
certain ma
how it wi
happen. Y
but that's
own you j

The third
desire…
for chang
so many t
didn't hav
people w
reasons a

One day I
to smoke
put this sn
another ci

quit.

The minute that you decide that's what you want, then that's exactly what you will do. The desire to change is a big part in changing how you're going to be celebrating life.

CHANGE YOUR THINKING... CHANGE YOUR LIFE!

THE LAW OF INCREASE

I am getting rich.
I am making others rich.
I am conferring blessings on all.

Increase is what you and I are seeking. Paul said: *I have planted Apollo waters but God gave the increase.* Corinthians 3:6. Increase is the urge of God within us seeking a fuller expression in all phases of our lives.

We are talking about spiritual economics. God gives the increase in the form of multi- plying the wheat grains a hundred fold… a thousand fold. When you plant something in the ground, then it multiplies. Likewise… whatever you plant in your mind, in the way of thoughts, feelings, imagination…that is increased in manifestation. From one seed… you have increase.

Think about corn. When you think about each one of those kernels of corn… it's really a seed. You plant the seed and you get a stalk of corn. Each stalk produces maybe 20 ears, and each ear produces maybe 500 more seeds. Think about that. Whatever you plant, has a way of increasing. Likewise… whatever you plant in your mind in the way of your thoughts, feelings and imagination, is always increased. Increase means the multiplication of whatever you are thinking and feeling. That's why we have to watch what- ever it is that we are thinking. This increase is the urge of God seeking expression through you.

God doesn't judge. This is probably one of the most important lessons we must learn. God has given us the power through the use of our minds to create whatever it is that we want. God does not say… he is thinking negative thoughts… he does not really want negative things to happen. I won't use the Law on this one. NO…God is the Law. Therefore… if you stay constantly in the negative, the law of increase is working for you just like it is for the people who are thinking about the good things that are going to happen.

The law of increase is the gift. How you and I use the law of increase is completely up to us. We plant a mental picture in our minds and we accompany that with a feeling of joy, completion, and happy ending. Then… what happens? We experience the joy, of the increase of that thought. You and I are the creative center and we can give an increase of love, wisdom and understanding to everyone that we meet. As we give, so do we receive. Let's start thinking about this: I am giving increase to everyone that I see. I am conferring them with riches. I expect them to prosper from what I say. This is the royal road to riches.

SELF-HYPNOSIS SCRIPT

THE INDUCTION

Make your body very comfortable. Relax. Close out everything from the outside world. Get a sense of inner quiet, peace, harmony into your being as you focus your eyes on any spot in a wide-open stare. Keep staring at that spot. You will find your eyes quickly get- ting tired. The lids get heavier and heavier. And now... close your eyes. Roll the eyeballs backwards. Take a deep breath. Let the eyes relax. Let the jaw relax. Let the shoulders go down. As your breath goes down slowly, everything goes into relaxation.

Now... imagine you have weights on your eyelids, making them feel so heavy and relaxed. Go deeper and deeper into this marvelous relaxed state. Your Sub-Conscious Mind is now fully forward... ready to accept positive, powerful suggestions.

THE MESSAGE

I like and respect myself, and others.

I know that I am a worthy and capable person. I look for ways to put myself and others up.

I show concern for the feelings of others. I write realistic, achievable goals.

All of my body systems are working in harmony to keep me healthy. I enjoy taking calculated risks to improve.

I call on HOLY SPIRIT for Guidance at all times. I am ever vigilant against the EGO thought system. I am grateful for my abundance.

I extend Love to all Loving Children of God. I enjoy sharing my abundance.

I write positive, goal-achieving affirmations each day with delight and enjoyment.

I am God's Son, complete and healed and whole, shining in the reflection of His Love. In me is His creation sanctified and guaranteed eternal life.

In me is love perfected, fear impossible, and joy established without opposite. I am the holy home of God Himself.

I am the Heaven where His Love resides.

I am His Holy Sinlessness Itself, for in my purity abides his Own.

THE AROUSAL

At each daily Self-Hypnosis practice, you will tell yourself: Next time, I will go deeper. And now… count from 5 to 1 for arousal. 5… remembering all that you need to remember. 4… take your suggestions deep within. Your Sub-Conscious Mind has locked them in… deeply embedded. 3… the blood begins to surge through your veins from the tip of your toes to the top of your head. All the organs are working in perfect harmony… perfect coordination. 2… coming up, feeling fine, coming alert, feeling wonderful. And… 1… wide awake, feeling great and full of energy… feeling fine

MAKING SELF-HYPNOSIS WORK

You now know that learning and practicing Self-Hypnosis is a natural and effective way to gain access to your Sub-Conscious Mind. It is a means of achieving your full potential.

When you are in the hypnotic state of consciousness, the Conscious Mind is not working and you can program any goal you wish into your Sub-Conscious Mind. You can use Self-Hypnosis to make your life more joyful, smoother, and better in every respect. The breaking of an addictive habit, or the accomplishing of any objective is a tremendous achievement. As a result of your accomplishment, you will find an upsurge of new confidence in your own inner being that will carry over into everything you do in life.

THE LAW OF CHANGE

Faith
Choice
Desire

We've all heard that there is nothing sure in life except change. Life is always changing and you and I can probably agree on this. The pain that we have experienced in life is when we've stayed too long with one thing that we knew we should leave. I look back on my life and every time I was in pain was when I stayed too long at the fair. Some- thing happens and it's wonderful and it feels really good and we say this is it. And then because life is change, life moves on and we stay. And then we begin to have pain in our life because we want to change our life.

We haven't learned that life does evolve and what was right at one time in our life is not necessarily right now. One of the laws for success is the law of change. Romans 2:12 says... *And be not conformed to this world but ye transformed by the renewing of your mind.* Isn't that telling you change your mind... change your life? Be not conformed to this world means that you're not locked in to whatever circumstances or situations or associations or challenges that exist in your life right now. You're not locked into that. You do not have to remain in that present condition. You can be transformed by the renewing of your mind. In other words... all you have to do is to change your mind and then of course you change your life.

What we think, we create. In other words you can change your life from whatever it is right now to anything you want it to be by changing your thinking.

The law of change has 3 fundamental aspects:

Faith

First of all we have to have faith in the law. Faith is defined as a firm belief or trust in something or someone generally before there's any proof about it. So it's a belief from which all doubt is removed, that's the difference between belief and faith. You have a biblical definition of faith which makes it really clear, and again this is where that comes from is Hebrews 11:1. *Now faith is the substance of things hoped for, the evidence of things not seen.* What this means is that in order to bring about the change in your life you must have faith that it's possible to do. No matter how negative any situation is that we're in, how absolutely overwhelming it may appear to be, if you have faith that things will get better then they're going to get better. Faith is that first step toward finding it. And if you have doubts that your life can change then you have faith in those doubts, you have faith that things are not going to work out and then you know what they are not going to work out. Faith works both ways.

Whatever it is that you have faith in that's what you bring about. If you have faith that you're not going to succeed or that this is never going to work for you, of course it doesn't, because your faith is bringing that about. If you have faith that it will work, if you have faith that life can get better, that things will happen, well of course they will.

Choice

Now the second aspect of this law of change is choice. People think they have no choice. They don't realize that every decision they make is a choice. Every opportunity, every challenge that we experience confronts us with a choice. We either choose a positive approach or we choose a negative approach. Even if we have no affirmative choice at all we do approach a mind set when we move into something.

In order for us to change our life for the better, we must affirmatively identify with a better life and what that better life means to us. It's easy to say I want a better life but have you thought about what a better life looks like to you?

You must decide what you want in your life and then you begin to focus on that. Now don't focus on how that's going to happen, just focus on the end result. See yourself living in the result of that choice. In other words, if you are choosing a success in a certain matter, see yourself living out that success and then the Universe will work out how it will bring it to you. It will work out the absolutely perfect avenue for that to happen. You and I think that we have to choose how things are going to happen to us but that's not the truth. The Universe has enough intelligence to work that out on its own you just live in end result.

Desire

The third aspect of the law of change is desire. The key ingredient for change is desire… a burning desire. Unless you have a really deep hunger, a burning desire for change, then it probably won't happen. I'm going to tell you that I quit smoking so many times, I was good at quitting, but then I would start back again because I didn't have a burning desire to quit. I quit for all the wrong reasons. I quit because people wanted me to quit, I quit because I thought I should quit, I quit for all those reasons and then I went back to smoking. I couldn't really quit.

One day I decided not that I shouldn't or it wasn't good for me. I decided I didn't want to smoke anymore. I really didn't want to smoke anymore. I decided I don't want to put this smoke in my lungs. This is crazy. The minute I made that decision, I never had another cigarette. I never even wanted another cigarette. But you see I had a desire to quit.

The minute that you decide that's what you want, then that's exactly what you will do. The desire to change is a big part in changing how you're going to be celebrating life.

CHANGE YOUR THINKING… CHANGE YOUR LIFE!

THE LAW OF INCREASE

I am getting rich.
I am making others rich.
I am conferring blessings on all.

Increase is what you and I are seeking. Paul said: *I have planted Apollo waters but God gave the increase.* Corinthians 3:6. Increase is the urge of God within us seeking a fuller expression in all phases of our lives.

We are talking about spiritual economics. God gives the increase in the form of multi- plying the wheat grains a hundred fold… a thousand fold. When you plant something in the ground, then it multiplies. Likewise… whatever you plant in your mind, in the way of thoughts, feelings, imagination…that is increased in manifestation. From one seed… you have increase.

Think about corn. When you think about each one of those kernels of corn… it's really a seed. You plant the seed and you get a stalk of corn. Each stalk produces maybe 20 ears, and each ear produces maybe 500 more seeds. Think about that. Whatever you plant, has a way of increasing. Likewise… whatever you plant in your mind in the way of your thoughts, feelings and imagination, is always increased. Increase means the multiplication of whatever you are thinking and feeling. That's why we have to watch what- ever it is that we are thinking. This increase is the urge of God seeking expression through you.

God doesn't judge. This is probably one of the most important lessons we must learn. God has given us the power through the use of our minds to create whatever it is that we want. God does not say… he is thinking negative thoughts… he does not really want negative things to happen. I won't use the Law on this one. NO…God is the Law. Therefore… if you stay constantly in the negative, the law of increase is working for you just like it is for the people who are thinking about the good things that are going to happen.

The law of increase is the gift. How you and I use the law of increase is completely up to us. We plant a mental picture in our minds and we accompany that with a feeling of joy, completion, and happy ending. Then… what happens? We experience the joy, of the increase of that thought. You and I are the creative center and we can give an increase of love, wisdom and understanding to everyone that we meet. As we give, so do we receive. Let's start thinking about this: I am giving increase to everyone that I see. I am conferring them with riches. I expect them to prosper from what I say. This is the royal road to riches.

I am getting rich.
I am making others rich.
I am conferring blessings on all.

If you are in business… you say to yourself: I'm getting rich and I'm making others rich. That is the way to succeed in business. As we give increase to others through our thoughts, then we become an instrument of God's love and truth and beauty. We claim these qualities and they are constantly flowing through others also. You begin to attract riches, friends, customers and marvelous experiences.

Life is a mirror. It mirrors back to us who we are. If we are one who is constantly giving the increase to others, then the increase is constantly being given to us. Opportunities are always knocking at everyone's door. We need to form a clear mental picture of what we want. We have to feel and know the power that we have within us. We have to realize that this law of increase is working in us night and day. It is a law of the mind. It is a law that was given for us to prosper.

What does prosper mean anyway? It literally means the law of increase. If you think one good thought, and it just remains one good thought, that's not the law of multiplying. If I think the good thought and then it multiplies, that's the law of increase… the law of prospering.

The law of prosperity works the other way as well. You can prosper in negative thinking. You can think negative thoughts, and they multiply. Yes… they do. You start out feeling bad…saying negative things in the morning and before the day is over you have so much negativity in your life. You say: I was feeling just a little bit bad this morning, and now I feel terrible. It has multiplied. No matter what we think… no matter what we feel… it increases. You and I become the responsible ones. It is my responsibility what I think. It is my responsibility how I live my life. It is my responsibility gauge what I want to increase.

There is no one who is responsible for my life except me. I have to cease blaming government, taxes, competition, world conditions. I can't do that. I cannot afford to do that because I have access to infinite mind and infinite riches.

How I think and feel can make me rich.
I attract and I increase.
It is my responsibility to do it.

THE LAW OF VISION

It's important to have an idea of where you want to go. Proverbs 29:18 says… *Where there is no vision, the people perish, but they that keep it the law, happy are they.* Let's talk about that. Where you have no vision of where you want to go with your life, you are miserable because you can't achieve something. It's kind of like ordering from a catalog. The Universe is going to send you whatever you order, but you need to be specific. You wouldn't pick up a Neiman Marcus catalogue and just write them a letter and say would you send me something. They would laugh at you. Well… the Universe has to know what to send you and it has to know what size… it has to know what color…. in other words you have to have a vision.

Your vision of the life that you would like to have, needs to be crystal clear in your mind. You need to see the vision in great detail. Internalize your vision through your senses… know how it looks… how it smells, how it feels… how it sounds… how it tastes… and so when you are fully experiencing your vision with your senses or your feeling nature, then you energize it and harmonize it with the universal force and make it happen in your life experience.

The law referred to in that second line of the scripture… *Where there's no vision the people perish, but they that keep it the law happy are they…* do you know what that's talking about? It's talking about really the first universal law of success… that law of thought and manifestation. What you recognize, or your vision that you energize with your feelings and what you energize through your feelings… you realize in your experience. Remember that? So the universal law of vision has really two aspects.

You must be specific and you must have imagination. To be specific about your vision… write it down… see it…understand what that means. You've got to have faith and you've got to know with assurance that your vision will be realized at the proper time. It is important to understand that. You must have a time table. The Universe has a time table. If we want something to happen so that it will be a success, then we have to do it in the Universes' time table. In other words you may want something in your life and you may clearly visualize yourself having it and you may decide that you need to have it now. It's like I don't want to have it tomorrow. I want to have it now. The Universe hears that and it brings it to you now. However… mentally and physically and spiritually you may not be ready… you may not have the consciousness to have it now.

Some things may need to happen in your life before you can keep it. So… you don't want to get what you want too soon because then you won't have the consciousness to keep it. You always say… in Divine Order, I want this in my life but I want it to be at the right time. Because you and I have a limited idea of what we can have, we don't want to limit ourselves by having a limited view of what's

THE LAW OF GROWTH

hing multiplies. We talk about… as you give… so do you receive. But… it's lied when it comes back to you. Think about this. What if you give ess? It comes back you… multiplied. Not just certain things are multiplied. verything is multiplied because one of the universal laws is constant growth. loes that mean to us on an individual level? It means that nothing stays the You and I are always changing. When we grow in understanding… or when w in misunderstanding… your life changes.

are always asking…*where are you from?* We are all from somewhere. I am oplin, Missouri. However… I don't live where I'm from. I make my annual nage back there, but…it's not the same. What's not the same about it is… me. ot the same. Therefore… I don't fit in. Is it their problem? NO. Is it my m? NO. It is simply a fact of life.

d I get romantic ideas about how things *used to be*. If we could plunk ourselves how they *used to be*… they probably would not be as great as we think we ber them. The point is… you can't go back. Thomas Wolfe wrote a play entitled: Iomeward Angel. One of the great lines in the play is: *You can never go home.* loes that mean? I can always go back to Joplin. I do it every year. But… I can't k to what I remember it being like. It doesn't exist anymore. Therefore… I can go home.

r for us to live life in the way that we need to live it… in order to get the most it… we have to acknowledge growth… nothing stays the same. Marriages tay the same. Jobs don't stay the same. People don't stay the same. Life t stay the same. If you spend a majority of your time bemoaning the fact that the way it used to be… the good old days… you just put yourself in an oy state, because it's not ever going to be that way.

something that I might have rejected in my early spiritual days because I ready to hear this. We have to realize that the Bible gives us instructions. We nterpreted them in an incorrect way. I can read something today and get a different meaning from it than when I was younger.

Old Testament… in the book of Isaiah… it says: *I am the Lord thy God, which th thee to profit which leadeth thee by the way thou shouldgo.*

say that in a different way: *The law of the Universe which you and I live .. will teach us how to be so that we can live a profitable life, and it will show direction in which we should go.*

w of the Universe that we live under is not just a law to be obeyed. It is a law stened to. That law is what we call Lord, or God. Four thousand years ago…

possible for us.

There is something that I always say when I do my goals.
important because you want to stress this to the Univer:
something better. In other words… you have a goal of what
but suppose that goal is not as far as you could go. People alw
and that's why I'm always talking about money… they g
understand. So… let's say that your goal in life is to have $
account. Now you're going to get that, if that's your goal… th
to have. But suppose it was possible for you to have $500,000
Would you want to give that up for the $50,000. You could sa
What good is that if you could have done 50 times better? So.
your goals down, always say this. This is the minimum of w
possible I want more… this or something better.

So you see… it's important that we have a goal, but let that goal b
maximum. Stretch yourself to the maximum. Do you see where
other words you stretch yourself to the maximum and put a goal
that you could possibly think of, but let that goal be the minimum
you more. You need a goal, we all need a goal, we all need som
just like the proverb says… those without a vision perish. If you'
you want… there is nothing left to do. You must have somewhe
You need to push yourself.

There are three types of goals.

Immediate Goals

Immediate goals are things that are closest and nearest. The:
things that you could do right now without much planning.

Intermediate Goals

Intermediate goals are your mid range goals. They are betwe
they're usually things that you have to complete before you can
goals.

Long Range Goals

Long range goals are from 3 to 5 years. This plan must be f
you achieve your immediate and you're working on you
usually things change. That causes your long range goals
information that you didn't have before you started the proces
information, we can have different choices. It's all about
flexibility.

You have to have a vision or you will

Every
multi
mean
NO. I
What
same.
we gr

Peopl
from
pilgri
I'm r
probl

You a
back
remer
Look
What
go ba
never

In ord
out o
don't
doesn
it's n
unhap

This
wasn
have
totall

In the
teach

Let n
under
us the

The l
to be

the people living in that day had not grown in consciousness to the capacity that we have grown. They were spiritually immature. In order to get it... they had to put skin onto God. They had to think of God as a person so that the people could get it. They understood what it meant when a father said... *I'll punish you if do that.* They could get that.

We have grown beyond that way of thinking. This Divine Law that we live under... it does not punish us. If we do not obey the law... we punish ourselves because of the law of growth. What we do... multiplies when comes back to us. The law says: *Do unto oters as you have them do unto you.* What that means is: *What you do unto others comes back to you... multiplied.* I am not being punished by that person. I have simply set up a set of circumstances that come back to me... multiplied. We have to watch what we do, because we are going to experience it coming back to us. It's going to it us like a brick.

The Law Of Growth is at work in the Universe.
Make it work for you.

CHAPTER TWO
THE 17 LIES... EXCUSES FOR FAILURE

Most people are afraid of failure. However... many of us are afraid of success. We create reasons why we are not going to succeed. In the process... we create our own failure. We some- how want to give a reason why it's not going to work... in case it doesn't work... so we don't feel like a fool. We know by studying the truth that what we think, believe and expect... creates the reality. So... we put those little lies out there to explain why we may not succeed. We are not saying that we are not going to succeed. But... in case we don't... it's not our fault. We pave the road ahead of us with these lies so that they will cushion us as we go along. Instead... it is creating the very failure that we don't want.

Wait until you see these 17 lies that we tell ourselves.

#1 LIE... IT'S WHO YOU KNOW

#2 LIE... IT'S MY DEFECT

#3 LIE... I'M TOO OLD FOR THAT

#4 LIE... I CAN'T

#5 LIE... I DON'T HAVE THE TIME

#6 LIE... THERE'S NOTHING I CAN DO

#7 LIE... I WORRY BECAUSE I CARE

#8 LIE... I'M SADDER BUT WISER

#9 LIE... HABITS ARE HARD TO BREAK

#10 LIE... PEOPLE REALLY UPSET ME

#11 LIE... WINNING THE LOTTERY WOULD SOLVE EVERYTHING

#12 LIE... THERE IS NO REASON TO STRIVE

#13 LIE... PEOPLE CAN AFFECT MY SELF-ESTEEM

#14 LIE... OH, FOR THE GOOD OLD DAYS

#15 LIE... THAT'S JUST THE WAY I AM

#16 LIE... STRUGGLE MAKES ME STRONGER

#17 LIE... I AM HELPLESS

#1 LIE... EXCUSE FOR FAILURE... IT'S WHO YOU KNOW

IT'S WHO YOU KNOW

How many of us have ever said that? If I knew the right people that could open the doors for me... I would be there in a minute. That is such a lie. In fact... I was watching a TV show recently. It was called... *In the shadow of singers*. It was about the children of singers who had made it in the business, and what a hard time they were having. Don't they know people who can open doors? Don't they already have name recognition? Of course they do. Have you ever wondered why children of famous people are not as famous as their parents? If the lie were true... **IT'S WHO YOU KNOW** that gets you there... they would be there.

Let's talk about the truth. The truth is who you are... not who you know. When I say... who you are... I am talking about your talents... your will to succeed... what it is within you that makes you who you are. If you use the term... **IT'S WHO YOU KNOW**... you are lacking the ingredient that is going to make you a success.

The difference between amateurs and professionals is easy to spot. You can watch some- one who has not quite made it yet and say... this one is going to make it, and this one is not. Some people just don't have the talent and it would not matter who they knew.

Cream rises to the top.

In the olden days when milk was delivered to the door, the milk was pasteurized, but it was not homogenized. The cream was on the top of the bottle and the skinny milk was underneath. You had to shake the bottle to get the milk evenly mixed. Hence the saying... cream rises to the top. That is what we are saying. If you have the talent... and you have the drive...like the cream... you will rise to the top.

A star in Hollywood is a star because they have star quality... not who they know. What is star quality? There are lots of beautiful girls. Some make it and some do not. The stars have something in them that says... pizzazz. The camera recognizes it and the public recognizes it. Suppose those people had stayed at home and said... I don't know anybody. There is no point in my even trying. That is an excuse for failure. That is a lie that we tell ourselves to keep ourselves down.

What does this all come down to? It comes down to... don't use that excuse to hold your- self back. When you believe that... what are you doing? You are believing that I am not going to make it because I don't know the right people. Well... guess what?

You are not going to make it because you believe a lie.

Let's get back to the truth. Whatever it is that we believe… we create. As we make these lies up to keep us sort of padded in our belief of non-success… we are literally creating the non-success. As we go through the 17 lies… make a list and say… I'm not going to do this anymore to myself because I can be anything if I believe that I can. If I truly believe that I can do this… then I can. I will no longer tell my self that it's who you know.

I have been talking about stars. Let's talk about in the office… or that book that you want to write… or that dream that you have never really attempted because this is the lie that you tell yourself. There is nothing worse than death… except one thing… the death of a possibility in your self that never really got to live. Everybody has dreams. Go for it now. What are you waiting on? You will never be any younger… and you are never too old. Do it now. If it is worth doing, and if you have what it takes to do it… it will work… it will. If it is the greatest song that was ever written… it will make it to the top. Maybe it is just the pleasure of doing something that you have always wanted to do.

Don't fall back on the lie that it's who you know.
NO… it's who you are.

Here is a little-known fact that will turn that thinking around.

This is the truth.

a total success at everything you have ever done. Let me explain. Every that you have ever had about what is going to happen to you… comes true. evailing idea that you have about yourself… you create… and it happens. ppen to think… there is something wrong with me… and you really believe idea that you have is the form that will be filled with Divine Substance, become your reality. Just as concrete is poured into a form…it hardens tever the form was… that is the reality. Divine Substance is just like the .

Your thought… the form… creates the reality.

Thoughts become things.

iefs about our abilities… the beliefs about what we can do are forms. The e fills it with Divine Substance… creating the reality. As long as we hold that we give the substance time to harden and stand on its own. We can look at ay… see… there was something wrong with me… that's why I didn't get ey even pointed it out to me. They even told me why I didn't get that.

That's why you are a success.

ter what your thoughts and ideas are… the Universe gives them to you. If k there is something wrong with you… you get it. If you think that you are ss… you get success. You pull to you exactly what you think.

would be someone who thinks one thing and gets another. That would not be ng who you are. We never think about validating ourselves in the negative. ve do it all the time… and with total success. We decide that this lie is true n the Universe validates us. Then… we can non-joyously say… *see*. People say… *see*… even if it's not good about themselves.

There is something wrong with me.
That is a lie.

s something absolutely perfect with you. You are created in the image of God. a child of God. You are whole and perfect in every way. There may be some rs that need cleaning up, but… that's not you. That is a behavior. We can behavior. Here is a quote from George Leonard: *Whatever your age, your ging, your education… what you are made of is unused potential.*

what you are. You are something waiting to become. You are perfecting your ion. Know that whatever you set out to do… and you believe you can do… n do.

#2 LIE... EXCUSE FOR FAILURE IT'S MY DEFECT

No matter what the problem is… there is a solution for begin out there. It begins in here. It begins in your minc yourself… how you think about life… your attitudes. This 17 lies that are holding us back from success. They are int so insidious. They are the little things that don't seem like camouflage themselves as the truth. When you scratch bel that there is nothing there.

THERE IS SOMETHING WRONG WITH ME..

Don't we think that? Who do you think put that in our hea They mean well. In the Midwest… we say… God bless 'e and say what you want to say. However… they did the be cases. They did not mean to cause any harm… in most case thinking that there is something wrong with me.

We can't lay all the blame on our parents. What abc experiences? Children are impressionable. It wasn't just other students could be cruel, also. When someone says sc to you… it's like a blow to the body. You can't see it on the and the bruise is inside, and it doesn't heal until we take a g that's not right. To say… there is something wrong with me to ourselves and it's not a defeat on the outside… it is just a w before it actually has a chance to begin. We somehow feel t

What about the church? I attended a Christening last month. what the Priest had to say. The words were all about this teen old… beautiful with a little white dress on… filled with si of the earth. Don't you think that little baby heard tha thinking… there is some- thing wrong with me. I've got to o order to achieve.

That's a lie.

The positive is: You are whole and perfect in every way. Some you are not who you are. Outside circumstances are not wh looking at yourself in the mirror this morning and saying… I a not defective.

You are thought Every If you it… th and wi and wh concret

The be Univer idea… it and that. T

No ma you th a succ

Failure valida But… and th love t

There You a behav chang *upbri*

That' perfe you c

#2 LIE... EXCUSE FOR FAILURE... IT'S MY DEFECT

No matter what the problem is... there is a solution for it. The solution does not begin out there. It begins in here. It begins in your mind... how you think about yourself... how you think about life... your attitudes. This is another episode of the 17 lies that are holding us back from success. They are interesting because they are so insidious. They are the little things that don't seem like lies... but they are. They camouflage themselves as the truth. When you scratch below the surface... you see that there is nothing there.

THERE IS SOMETHING WRONG WITH ME... IT'S MY DEFECT

Don't we think that? Who do you think put that in our head... our loving parents. They mean well. In the Midwest... we say... God bless 'em. Then you can go on and say what you want to say. However... they did the best they could... in most cases. They did not mean to cause any harm... in most cases. But... we came away thinking that there is something wrong with me.

We can't lay all the blame on our parents. What about those early school experiences? Children are impressionable. It wasn't just the teachers... but the other students could be cruel, also. When someone says something mean-spirited to you... it's like a blow to the body. You can't see it on the outside, but the wound and the bruise is inside, and it doesn't heal until we take a good look at it and say... that's not right. To say... there is something wrong with me... is a way that we talk to ourselves and it's not a defeat on the outside... it is just a way of killing something before it actually has a chance to begin. We somehow feel that we are defective.

What about the church? I attended a Christening last month. I listened carefully to what the Priest had to say. The words were all about this teeny little child... 6 weeks old... beautiful with a little white dress on... filled with sin... worthless... scum of the earth. Don't you think that little baby heard that? So... we grow up thinking... there is some- thing wrong with me. I've got to overcome something in order to achieve.

That's a lie.

The positive is: You are whole and perfect in every way. Somebody's thoughts about you are not who you are. Outside circumstances are not who you are. How about looking at yourself in the mirror this morning and saying... I am not a failure... I am not defective.

Here is a little-known fact that will turn that thinking around.

This is the truth.

You are a total success at everything you have ever done. Let me explain. Every thought that you have ever had about what is going to happen to you… comes true. Every prevailing idea that you have about yourself… you create… and it happens. If you happen to think… there is something wrong with me… and you really believe it… that idea that you have is the form that will be filled with Divine Substance, and will become your reality. Just as concrete is poured into a form…it hardens and whatever the form was… that is the reality. Divine Substance is just like the concrete.

Your thought… the form… creates the reality.

Thoughts become things.

The beliefs about our abilities… the beliefs about what we can do are forms. The Universe fills it with Divine Substance… creating the reality. As long as we hold that idea… we give the substance time to harden and stand on its own. We can look at it and say… see… there was something wrong with me… that's why I didn't get that. They even pointed it out to me. They even told me why I didn't get that.

That's why you are a success.

No matter what your thoughts and ideas are… the Universe gives them to you. If you think there is something wrong with you… you get it. If you think that you are a success… you get success. You pull to you exactly what you think.

Failure would be someone who thinks one thing and gets another. That would not be validating who you are. We never think about validating ourselves in the negative. But… we do it all the time… and with total success. We decide that this lie is true and then the Universe validates us. Then… we can non-joyously say… *see*. People love to say… *see*… even if it's not good about themselves.

There is something wrong with me.
That is a lie.

There is something absolutely perfect with you. You are created in the image of God. You are a child of God. You are whole and perfect in every way. There may be some behaviors that need cleaning up, but… that's not you. That is a behavior. We can change behavior. Here is a quote from George Leonard: *Whatever your age, your upbringing, your education… what you are made of is unused potential.*

That's what you are. You are something waiting to become. You are perfecting your perfection. Know that whatever you set out to do… and you believe you can do… you can do.

Let go of this lie… **THERE IS SOMETHING WRONG WITH ME**. It's not the truth. Don't even go there. That is a voice of fear… a passive fear. It is opposite of your sole purpose. We have a reason to be here. We have a Divine reason to be on this planet. Don't let any of these psychological fears keep us from what we were created to be. Don't let internal defeat… quitting before we even begin… stop us from achieving our potential.

Life is good.
You deserve to celebrate every bit of it.

#3 LIE... EXCUSE FOR FAILURE... I'M TOO OLD FORTHAT

This is another lie that holds us back. Like the others… it is not the truth. We convince ourselves that this is the truth so that we have an excuse not to succeed at something. This is one that I really identify with, and maybe you will, too:

I'M TOO OLD FOR THAT

That is an increasing situation that we have to deal with. Why… because our population is getting older. I am part of that. I remember when I was a kid. My aunts and uncles, who were my age now, they were old. We sort of fuss about this youth-culture that we live in… which came about after the '50's. What it has done for us is that it has not just promoted youth for the young people… it has promoted youth for every age. I am younger than my aunts and uncles were when they were my age. I remember them. I remember how they looked. I remember how they acted. There is almost no similarity. We are getting younger. Yet… the numbers carry the same psychological weight now as they did then.

I am thinking that the new 60 is the old 40. Why not? People died at 55. That was it. Very few people lived to 70. Hey… I'm just getting going. I am not even shaped like those people used to be shaped. They were wrinkled and had thinning hair or no hair. My aunts wore funny little corsets. They looked like little pigeons in the front. The bodies are younger now. So… that excuse… I'm too old for that… simply does not fly anymore. It's a lie.

People who are now in so-called middle-age now… they can do anything someone in their 30's and 40's can do. Look at the people in the gym… lifting weights… times are different. Are you telling yourself… I'm too old for that? Age is a state of mind. It really is. You are as old as you think you are.

In the Fall, we get inundated with Flu Season information on the radio and on the TV. It's Flu Season. Then… all of a sudden… everybody gets the Flu. Why? I don't think the flu germs decide… it's our season. It's time now for us to do our thing. NO. I think a lot of it has to do with the fact that we expect to get the flu at a certain time of the year. So… we know the mind-body connection… and what we expect to happen… happens in our bodies. If you tell yourself… I'm too old for that… well… do the math. You know what will happen.

YOU WILL BE TOO OLD FOR THAT.
That's a lie.

When my friend, Reverend Maureen, decided to go to Ministerial School, she had to go to 2 years of school on campus… 3 years of at home study before that… before she could even apply. She applied. You cannot imagine the number of people that came to her and said… "Maureen… you don't want to do that. You are gong to be 55 years old when you graduate." She said… "I'm going to be 55 anyway. I might as well be 55 doing something I know I am supposed to do and be 55 or not."

We are going to continue to age.
It's never too late.

Do you want to start Yoga? You say… I'm not limber like those people are. Well... start Yoga and 5 years from now… you probably will be. The whole key is… BEGIN. Begin now. It's never too late. You're never too old to do what you want to do. Grandma' Moses didn't begin painting until she was in her 80's. Suppose she had thought… Oh… I'm too old for that. NO. It's a mind-set.

I know you are thinking about something right now that you did not do when you were younger. When you say… I'm too old to do that… I don't necessarily mean senior citizens. What about people in their 30's that did not get a college education? You say… why don't you go to college now? They say… I cant. I'm too old for that. WRONG. You can do it now. If you feel that there is something that you feel that you have missed when you were younger… do it now.

Yeah but… they have already done it… they will be way ahead of me. You don't know that. You may go and leap ahead of them. You'll never know until you do it.

Remember… it's lie.
I'M TOO OLD FOR THAT

You are never too old to begin. You will progress. The sad thing is… that if you never try it… you'll never know. The saddest phrase in the English language is… IF ONLY. If only… I had done that. It is a matter of getting over the mind-set. It is a matter of deciding what you want to do and doing it. I don't care what age you are.

You are so fortunate because you have a Higher Power… you have a Higher Self that can help you with what ever it is that you want to do. Don't just depend on your physical self. Call in your Higher Self. I want to do this. Show me how I can do this now. You will be so surprised at the answer that you will receive. Don't let life slip by you.

Human beings are the only species that have to be encouraged to live. Think about that. We are always saying… get off your duff and live. Do something. People in retirement homes who seem to be confined to wheel chairs get stronger and get out of their wheel chairs when they begin working with weights. If we are not building… we are dying. Every time you say… I'm too old for that… you are driving a nail into that coffin.

IT'S TIME TO BE CELEBRATING LIFE.

#4 LIE... EXCUSE FOR FAILURE... I CAN'T

We use this lie all the time. You say... well... what's wrong with that? When you can't do something... you can't do it. I'm not talking about walking a tight-rope strung between two buildings. I can't at the moment. I suppose I could do that if I worked at it. I'm talking about the way we use... I can't. What it does... it robs us... it makes us victims instead of allowing us to be in control of our lives.

An example might be: Someone asks me to meet them for lunch, and I say... I can't do that because my car is in the shop. That's a lie. I could take the bus. "I can't" puts me in the victim position. What would be more appropriate is: I choose not to do that because my car is in the shop. That is the truth. If I really wanted to go... I could. This way... I am not going by choice... I am being honest. I am taking responsibility in letting the per- son know that I choose not to go. I am not a victim.

"I can't" takes power away from us. Anything that takes power away from us... makes us a victim... we resent it. Suppose we say... I can't because I have to go to work. Now... I don't like work because it makes me a victim. The point is... you don't have to go to work. You choose to go to work because it allows you to pay the bills. So... it would be more appropriate to say... I choose not to do that because I choose to go to work. Now... you are not a victim and you do not resent going to work. So... if we switch out that lie of... "I can't"...to "I choose not to"... it prevents resentment.

Resentments build up animosities and that blocks us from creative power.

Think about how you use... "I can't". I can't afford this. Actually you could. What you might say instead is... "I choose to allocate my resources differently." Once again... no resentment. You do not need to be Poor Pitiful Peter. As we begin to change... "I can't" to "I choose to do something else"... that puts it in a different light... a totally different mind-set. "I can't"... disables us in so many ways. There is always a *because*. That *because* becomes artificial. It is not the reason. It is really because I choose not to.

The thing that really sets me on edge is when people know that they need to change something and they say... "I can't". You know what is happening when you do that. What you are actually saying is..."I choose not to do that". For example...I can't lose weight. I can't exercise. I can't quit smoking. NO. That's a lie. You could if you wanted to. You say...I don't like to say...I choose not to that because that makes me responsible. That's where we get right down to it. You are responsible... like it or not. These are your choices. In order to eek out that little dab of guilt we have about not taking responsibility… we say…"I can't" instead of saying… "I am choosing not to do this".

When we say… "I choose"… that puts the power back in our court. When I receive an invitation that I do not want to accept… I say… "Thank you, but…I don't do that. I use my time differently." That's the truth. However… when we make excuses… we are putting bad feelings on those things we are blaming. Take the responsibility for yourself.

When someone tells me…I can't do that… I do not buy that. I will buy… I don't want to do that. I know that if you want to do it… you can do it. Just using… "I can't"… is the lie that we get accustomed to and it serves us very well. It's a really good excuse.

Don't say…"I can't"…anymore. Say…"I choose not to do that. I don't want to do that". You will not believe how much power you will feel.

Take your power back.

#5 LIE... EXCUSE FOR FAILURE ... I'D LOVE TO DO THAT, BUT I DON'T HAVE THE TIME

How many times have you said that? That is a lie. People say… there's never enough time. That's a lie. I really want to do that … but I don't have the time. Let's see what you are really saying because neither of those is true. It's not true that you really want to do that. If you really wanted to do that… you would make the time. So… you really don't want to do that. When you say there is not enough time… you are convincing yourself that it is something that is going to be a hindrance to yourself.

There is always enough time. What is lacking is a desire and a sense of purpose. What would be the truth to say would be: "I wish I wanted to do that enough to make the time." That does not mean that you have not had a fleeting desire to do it. That is the problem right there. You and I get totally overwhelmed with society today. The reason is we have too many things going on… too many irons in the fire.

It seems like that there is never enough time, when actually… we are not accomplishing anything. We are using our precious time to be overwhelmed. So… at the end of the time period… we haven't done anything. Of course we feel overwhelmed. We are trying to think about too many things every day. We are not focused. Thinking about too many things every day… we never have enough real time to develop anything.

Here is what you do: Slow down… do less… accomplish more. Did you know that you can accomplish more if you slow down and do less? Here is a quote from Sir Isaac New- ton. When he was asked how did you discover gravity? He said: *You would have done that, too, if that's all you ever thought about every day and every night*. That man was focused. He had a purpose.

Our problem is not that there is not enough time. The problem is… you and I don't have the strength to do. Strength comes from slowing down and choosing what to focus on. If you and I are scattered and non-focused… we are spreading our strength out in all directions and there is not enough left to do any one thing. We have to learn how to be strong. Real strength comes from slowing down and choosing what to focus on. Until then… you are going to worry equally about every problem You are going to take every phone call… you are going to ponder every piece of mail with equal energy. That is not a strong way to live.

As we do one slow thing at a time… we become focused and we find that we do have the time. I have done this and it is almost as though time stands still. Get focused on what you are doing and complete it. Don't do half a job and then do another half a job. NO. Complete your jobs one at a time. Multi-tasking zaps your strength. Only think about one thing at a time. That way, you are completely focused.

While I am writing this book… do you think that I am thinking about what I am going to be doing after the book is published? NO. My attention is devoted to what I am doing right now… 100 percent. I am completely focused on what I am doing… right now. I have to be careful that I don't get so focused and carried away that I go on forever. We need to focus on what we are doing at the time we are doing it… bring everything we have into the situation. We bring all of our resources into play.

Remember what I said about opening every piece of mail and giving everything the same energy? We need to learn that it is OK to get mail that we never even open. Personal letters… I always open. I am talking about that stuff that you get in the mail that you can tell that it may be a good cause and all that. But… you do not need to let it occupy your time or energy. Why should I spend 3 minutes reading it? Toss it… toss it… toss it. After I scan what I have decided to keep… I may end up tossing that, too. I only take into my office that mail that I am going to answer. What if I sat down and looked at all of it the same way? You can't do that… not with all the mail that comes in every day. I hope that you don't read all your e-mails, either.

You cannot be concerned about… am I giving this too much time? NO. Make a decision. You and I are powerful people. We need to make decisions. That way… we can stay focused on what we have made a decision to give our time to. We can accomplish so much more. It is almost Zen-Buddhist. They have a practice about being mindful…to be aware. If you are touching a book… you are totally aware of how the book feels. If you are drinking coffee… you totally taste every swallow. You feel the cup on your lips. It's being totally aware of everything that we do. When we forget time and we focus on the situation… all of a sudden… time is on our side. I would love to do that…but I don't have the time… has no meaning. First of all… you don't want to do it. And… you do have the time. Those are 2 lies that hold us back.

#6 LIE... EXCUSE FOR FAILURE... THERE IS NOTHING I CAN DO

Boy… do we use that one. This is what happens to us. We wake up in the morning, think of some event, and we say… well… there is nothing I can do about that. Then… all of a sudden there is a crisis that comes up involving that event. If the crisis is big enough… somehow… all that gets changed. Funny how that is. Before the crisis hit… we tell our- selves… there is simply nothing I can do about that. When we tell ourselves that… we feel like we have more control. You ask… saying that creates control? Sure it does. Things do not change. We change. Henry David Thoreau said that. So… why do we waste so much of our time wishing that things would change? We spend so much time hoping that things are going to be different. Most of us do not progress past that point. Wishing is a way to remove ourselves from reality.

Wishing that something would change… is really avoidance. We are lying to the soul in an unconscious attempt to avoid changing. When you say, "that's how it is…there is nothing I can do"… that is a lie. There is something you can do about the situation. But…it's not about the situation. It's about your attitude about the situation. That is all that life is. Life is a series of perceptions. We have a perception about how something is. We can change that perception.

Nothing succeeds like failure. Why? When we say… that's not going to work… what we really mean is… it might not change things. But… things don't change. You and I change. You can wake up with an attitude of… I can do… and everything gets done that day. Or… you can wake up with an attitude of… there is nothing I can do… and nothing gets done. What is the catalyst there? What is happening in each of those situations? It is our attitude about what can be accomplished.

Here is a good quote. This fellow founded IBM. "If you want to double your success rate... double your failure rate." It is fear of failure that prevents success. You and I get locked into the fact that there is nothing that we can do. So… we don't do anything and that sets in a victim attitude. There is that word *victim* again. A victim attitude never gets anything done. A victim attitude is what keeps us from our truth.

Aren't we designed in the image and likeness of God? Don't we have within us the power to create our reality? But… we focus on failure. Then what happens is… we create our own failure through our focus on it. Whatever you and I focus on… becomes our reality. Deepak Chopra says… "To worry is to pray for what you don't want." Prayer is every- thing we think. That's how we communicate with the universal law of creation. What we think goes out and comes back to us. Isaiah says...*What comes from my mouth...does not return to me void.*

When we say... there is nothing I can do about that... think again. The minute I change... everything changes. The minute that I have a different attitude... a different perception... the situation changes. Give that a try. If you are looking at a situation that you see no way around it... look at it from every angle. You can definitely say... "I see what not to do with it." But...don't say... there is nothing I can do. There is always something you can do. What s that? Change your attitude about what you see. That is the one thing that you can always do, I don't care what it is. Change the attitude about what you see. Say to yourself... everything changes when I change. So... saying... there is nothing I can do about this... is a lie.

If you change... it changes.

You say... it really doesn't change. Don't you understand that it wasn't concrete to begin with? We think that everything in this world is solid and fixed. That is not true. It is fluid. Life is energy. That is a metaphysical truth. It forms in a reality according to the way we see it. You must believe something... and then you see it.

Believing is seeing.

We used to have that backwards. You must believe and then it forms into what you believe. So... changing your perception... changes the situation. You say... how am I going to change? What do I change? Only you know that. That changes with each situation. The prayer can be: *Show me what I need to see here.* It may even be: *What is the lesson I need to learn here.* Why does this keep showing up in my life? Could it be that the Universe says... I am going to keep giving you this until you get it? Maybe it was attitude that needed to be changed to begin with.

Life is a classroom.

Life never presents us with anything that we cannot handle. So... saying... there is nothing I can do about this... is not true. I can change. Things don't change. You change... it changes.

#7 LIE...
EXCUSE FOR FAILURE...
I WORRY BECAUSE I CARE

"To worry is to pray for what you don't want."
Deepak Chopra

Worrying is probably the most unproductive thing that we could ever do. We get con- fused between worry and empathy. I can empathize with you if you are going through a problem. I can feel it and know how it would be. I am sorry that you are going through it. But… I'm not going to worry about it. People think that worrying about something shows their concern, or that they love you. If you don't help them worry… they accuse you of not caring. Now... we have worrying and caring confused.

If you are concerned about something… then do something about it. But… don't worry about it. The Serenity Prayer comes to mind:

God give me the serenity to accept the things I cannot change,
The courage to change the things I can,
And the wisdom to know the difference.

Notice that it doesn't say any thing in there about worrying. NO. Worrying is a waste of time. We worry because that is what we do to avoid taking action. As you worry… it becomes a habit. That is how you occupy your mind… it's a habit. Worrying becomes the activity. Instead of worrying… we should take the activity. Or… give me the wisdom to know the difference. If I can't do anything about something… what does worrying accomplish? NOTHING. If you can do something about it… then… do it. But… do not spend your time worrying about something that you cannot do anything about. Does that you mean you don't care? NO. Most people worry about things that they cannot do any- thing about. God help people that worry about things that they *can* do something about… but… they don't. That is where the sad part comes in.

Worrying becomes a habit. We become worry-warts. We worry about everything. Then… we become sanctimonious with our worrying. Some people worry because they don't have anything else to do… no life of their own… nothing to take up their time. Situations become a big deal because they have time on their hands.

A good way to get out of the worrying habit is… every time you find yourself worrying about something… take action… that minute… any action. You must do something every time you find yourself worrying. That is a great way to teach yourself not to worry… particularly if you are a procrastinator.

When you tell yourself… I worry because I care… that is not the truth. That's a lie we have told ourselves. Remember… if you care… you would do something about it. Worrying doesn't do it. We have told ourselves that if we worry… we are doing something about it. That is not the action to take.

On a metaphysical level, to worry is to pray for what you don't want. Remember… everything that you put out there… comes back to you. Isaiah says... *My words do not come back to me void.* That goes for our thought, also. So… every time we worry about something… we are making sure that it happens. So… if I care about you, I will suggest that you change your attitude… wisdom to know the difference. Let the thought that I put out… be the thoughts that I want to have come back to me.

This goes back to affirmative prayer. We see it rightly. We see the perfect outcome. We stay in that. If you want to occupy your mind instead of worrying about a situation, you need to picture it as the perfect outcome, however that looks to you. Sometimes we don't know what the perfect outcome is. What we can see is the result of a perfect outcome. We can go there. We see contentment, harmony, prosperity, whatever. As we see that… that is what the reality becomes.

So… if you really care about someone… and you can't do anything physically for them… see it rightly for them. See it as God sees it. See it perfectly done. That is the way we pray. Worrying is a form of prayer. It is praying for what you do not want to happen. If you worry about someone… it's not because you care. If you cared… you would do something. If you cared… you would see it rightly.

When you worry… you are acting pitiful. You are acting in the victim mentality. We need to stay out of the victim mentality. If we give victim mentality to the Universe… it will give us back what we give to it. It is a mirror... a reflection.

The Universe reflects back to me what I am.
If I am a worrier… it gives me something to worry about.

To worry is to pray for what you don't want.

#8 LIE... EXCUSE FOR FAILURE... I'M A SADDER BUTWISER PERSON

This is an old saying that we have heard and have come to believe. It is a lie. It flies right in the face of happiness. It implies that if I am a sadder and wiser person... then if I am happy. I must be a fool. Nobody wants to be a fool. This is how it goes. People often take that on as a way of being because it is kind of easy. It feels like the safest way to be. No one can stifle your enthusiasm if you don't have any. That carries over into other parts of our lives. In other words... if I don't ever fall in love... I can't get hurt. It is like opting to not live so that life won't be taken away from you. It's like saying... I don't want to be born because I don't want to die. We make sadness a virtue if we say... I'm sadder and wiser.

Let's get this out of the way. I'm not talking about being sad because something happened to your pet... you are going through a divorce... a loved one died. People always come up with that. People who want to defend terminal sadness always come up with a reason that they want to stay sad. They say... are you telling me it is wrong to be sad when so and so dies? NO. I'm not saying that. Use some common sense. I'm talking about those people who have made sadness a way of life. You may say... well... that's not me. But...think about it. Think about how many days you opt to not show any enthusiasm because you are afraid of what might happen. You are afraid you may be wrong.

People have been known to play dead to save their lives. On the battlefield, soldiers play dead, lying motionless, hoping that the enemy will assume them to be dead so that they will not be killed. People do not have to be on the battlefield to play dead... to show no sign of life. Have you ever been in a meeting where many of the attendees were playing dead? They were keeping a low profile... like soldiers lying on the battlefield... allowing a few daring souls to carry the day. They just sit there... showing no participation... no enthusiasm. They did not want to commit themselves in front of their boss... risking disapproval. A person who does not speak out is a sad person. Have you ever been around people who speak so soft that they just barely murmur? That person was probably put down by his parents when he was young. He has established a way of speaking so that it would not be noticed. That is away of playing dead.

In order to be a sadder but wiser person... we are going to have to dumb-down our minds because it is natural to show animation. So... these people appear stupid, because they don't want to risk looking stupid. They bring about exactly what they are trying to pre- vent. That is stupid. People who do this... lie low in these situations... are usually lying low in their lives. A Zen writer said: *How you do anything is how you do everything.* If you are going to play dead so that life doesn't shoot you… you are missing out on life. It is much better to be excited. Be excited about life. It doesn't matter if you don't fit the mold. Who is the mold? Probably some sad-sack. Create your own mold. The word enthusiasm comes from the Greek word *enfios* which means… the God within. If you approach life with enthusiasm… it means that you are displaying the God within.

So…when you say… I'm a sadder but wiser guy… that is a lie. Sadder and wiser is actually an oxymoron. Those two words do not go together. Suppose you and your co-workers are working on a project, and the boss is not around. During the working, you get the giggles. Now… around the corner comes the boss. Everybody stops laughing and goes back to being somber. The inspiration comes when you are in that smiley… giggly mood.

Sadder but wiser is totally untrue.
Live life today with great enthusiasm.
That is celebrating life.

#9 LIE... EXCUSE FOR FAILURE... HABITS ARE HARD TO BREAK

The longer I have had a habit... the harder it is to break... is a lie.

This is a damaging lie. It stops all change. Once you have told yourself that you can't break the habit... there is nothing you can do about it... there isn't. For example... people say... have had this habit too long to even consider letting it go. Everybody knows that the longer you have a habit... the harder it is to break. Well... that is not the truth. Our perception determines our behavior. If few perceive ourselves to be non-smokers... then it would never occur to us to want a cigarette. If we perceive ourselves to be a smoker... we live out that perception. That's what the Sub-Conscious Mind does. It pictures things and that becomes our automatic way of acting. That becomes our truth... our relative reality. The minute the perception changes... the truth changes.

The key to eliminating the hold that the habit has on you... is to change the perception. That is accomplished by re-programming the Sub-Conscious Mind. When we see our selves as non-smokers, non-drinkers, non-over-eaters, the change happens immediately. That then becomes our new habit. Change happens instantly. Habits take time. The change of habit can take place only if your want it to. It will not work if you are doing it for somebody else. Being a non-smoker is different from being a smoker running around without a cigarette. The difference is... how does your Sub-Conscious Mind perceive it?

When you have developed the new habit... the old habit is completely forgotten... no more desire... no more craving for the old way of thinking. You need to picture your new habit as being your new reality with constant, daily re-enforcement... daily practice. This is identical to affirmative prayer. Give thanks for what is already yours. The intention is fulfilled. You see yourself as you want to be. If you can picture that... and say... this is who I am... the Sub-Conscious Mind will hear your affirmation and get you there.

You do not picture yourself as a smoker and then try to quit. That will not work. Picture yourself as a non-smoker. That will work. You will be as you picture yourself. If you picture yourself as a thin person... you will become that picture. Look through a magazine and picture things that you want and make a collage. That is called a Treasure Map. You will be surprised when your Treasure Map begins to manifest as your reality. You can cut out pictures of bodies that you admire, a house that catches your eye, a car that you have always wanted. You will be surprised how your pictures become your reality.

Telling ourselves… the longer I have had a habit… the harder it is to break… is a lie. If you picture yourself, constantly, the way you want to be… you have created a clear intention. The deeper the intention… the stronger the sense of purpose. Practice takes it down to the soul.

All that matters is that you are ready for a new perception and purpose. Do you really want to change? That is the key. Using… I can't change… is an excuse. Don't tell your- self that you have had this habit too long. That's a lie. How do we confirm a perception? If there is a new perception of ourselves… we do it with practice… repetition. After a while… the new habit sets in and begins confirming itself… giving us confidence in our new reality. Changing is nothing. Maintaining the change… requires reinforcement.

People change in a nano-second. People go from a smoker to a non-smoker in an instant. Whatever that habit is that you want to change… whether you have done it for 3 weeks or 20 years… the process is exactly the same. How long we have been doing something means nothing. The action that we take to create a new perception… that means every- thing. It goes along with affirmative prayer… praying rightly. Pray believing… and it is yours. That is a law of the Universe. You must tell yourself… I don't do that anymore. I used to do that, but I don't do it anymore. I don't do that. Keep telling yourself… that's not who I am. The minute that you tell that to your Sub-Conscious Mind… it believes it and it acts on it.

The longer I have a habit… the harder it is to break… is a lie.

#10 LIE... EXCUSE FOR FAILURE... PEOPLE REALLY UPSET ME

That is not the truth. We are upsetting ourselves. You say… well… if he had not have said that… I wouldn't be upset. Think about that. You have to admit that you are lying to your- self about the situation every time it happens. That is not an easy one. Every time you get upset… every time you start pointing the finger… you need to say to yourself… every time I point this finger… there are 3 pointing back at me. Majority rules. I am the who that upsets myself. Think about that. No one has the power to upset you. We can only upset ourselves.

When something happens… you and I put a spin on it. We decide at the moment… is this a good thing… is this a bad thing. Not only do we have a spin we put on it… but it brings up every situation in our life that was similar to that. In other words… we have a bank of incidents that we can roll out and say… this fits in this category. This is an upsetting thing that is happening. I am upset.

We have gone through a process of thought. When we are upset… we are thinking of sending those thoughts to our body. Something has to happen between what somebody said and our being upset. That thing that happens is a process of thought. We can only get upset when we think… this is upsetting me.

An incident happens, and it just an incident. Don't think of something that has happened that has upset you. Just think of an incident. Let's say that I am waiting for the elevator. The elevator door opens and someone rushes in and almost knocks us down getting in ahead of us. That's what happened. I have some people go ballistic over that. Some people say… he sure is in a hurry and calmly walk in. The same thing happened to two people. What was the difference there? The person who went ballistic could tell you with a very straight face and with a sincere mind… this person really upset me. That really upsets me when something like that happens. Well… that incident did not upset that per- son. What that person thought about that is what upset him.

Therefore… what happens in our mind… sets off feelings What you think creates what you feel. If you think something is good… then you get a feeling of good. If you think something is bad… then you get a corresponding feeling. So… you say… I'll go along with that. But suppose if that had not happened… I would not have been set on this path. Well… that is where our self-control comes in. There is no way you and I can control what is going to be happening to us today. But... we can control how we react to what happens to us. That is going to affect how we feel about it.

Once we begin thinking correctly… that we are actually upsetting ourselves… then it will also feel that way. It will no longer feel like people are upsetting us. We will begin to understand where the feelings are coming from. If we begin to think differently… then we begin to feel differently. Then you begin to understand that it is something that we think that is upsetting us.

Let's take the same scenario… that person that was so upset… that person who went ballistic on the elevator. Suppose that person had just won the Lottery. Do you think that for one instant…f or one nano-second … that a person running in front of him to get in the elevator would have upset him? NO… NO… NO.

If you are already in a happy frame of mind… someone could run over your foot and you would smile at them because you are thinking happy thoughts. We have just taken the power away from the upset. It's the thought that makes us happy or not happy. It's the thought in our own mind.

I said that you and I bring up situations. Well… we do. Those situations… those banks of situations that we are ready to bring up at any moment… those buttons that when pushed, bring up a situation… you get hooked… you go into automatic think-feel. You don't even know what the truth is. You don't even know why you are mad. All of a sudden… they pushed your button and you shot right into your think-feel mode. You can- not stop those things that come from other people. What we have to do is to eliminate the buttons. Eliminate the hooks. We need to become like a cue ball… so smooth that nothing hooks on it. Nothing sticks on it. Now… we are taking the responsibility back to our- selves. It is all happening inside of us.

People do not upset us. We have thoughts that upset us. People can trigger those thoughts. We have to do something about the trigger. What is the difference between thinking and feeling? Feeling is what you get from thinking the way you do. If you stop thinking that somebody has upset you… you will stop feeling that someone has upset you.

Don't fall into the trap.
People do not upset you.
It's a lie.

#11 LIE... EXCUSE FOR FAILURE... WINNING THE LOTTERY WOULD SOLVE EVERYTHING

SPIRITUAL GIFTS

Before we get into this... I want to make it perfectly clear that everything we have said about the spiritual gifts from God still applies. You do not have to ask for prosperity, perfect health, perfect relationships. These and all of your other needs are already yours without the asking. You do not need to do anything to *earn* them. They are your rightful inheritance. They are given to you by the grace of God. The definition of grace is an *unearned* gift. All you have to do is say... "Thank you God."

EARTHLY GIFTS

One of the greatest disservices we could do for someone may be to give them a huge sum of **$$$**... unearned **$$$.** That includes the Lottery. Often times... we look at the Lottery ticket and we plan on how we are going to spend the **$$$** before the numbers are even drawn. That is unearned **$$$.** In this civilization... it is the way we keep score. Think about it. If someone says... what are you worth... we immediately go to the monetary worth instead of the spiritual worth. People do not have a high esteem of them- selves if they have all this **$$$** and they don't feel like they earned it.

You may say... it wouldn't bother me. That's what we might all think... now. However... too many people have won the Lottery... only to have it ruin their lives. I won't tell you that I would not take the **$$$** if I won the Lottery, but... I do understand that won't solve my problems. Winning the Lottery is just like adding decimal points to your problems. You will still have the same problems. They will just become bigger.

It is interesting how people treat people who have acquired unearned **$$$.** They say... give me some. After all... you didn't earn it. That feeling of resentment has broken up families.

On the other hand... something interesting happens to us when we do it ourselves... when we get down into the nitty-gritty and solve the problem. For instance... someone who has had a difficult time with math who works on it and works on it until he is proficient feels a great sense of accomplishment. The same goes for someone who becomes a proficient musician, dancer, singer. No one can just hand the accomplishment to them. They must do it themselves by determination, hard work, and practice. You can pay someone to be the teacher… but in the final analysis… you have to do the work. If you do not… it doesn't matter how much **$$$** you have to pay the teacher. That gives us the self-esteem to move along. That is the measure of how much we are worth. Money cannot buy happiness, success, and accomplishment.

What is the Lottery, anyway. You say… it is about winning a lot of **$$$.** You also think that if I win… I will be wealthy… everyone will look up to me. You may be able to live high on the hog… you may be able to buy your way in. But… you are not going to feel good about yourself. The thing that makes us feel good is self-esteem... to earn what you get. I am not just talking about $$$. This applies to everything in life. What about the boss's son being promoted even though he may not have the ability… nepotism. He does not have the self-esteem… the respect… because he did not *earn* it.

Studies have been conducted regarding Lottery winners. A year or 2 later… they are not any happier than they were before. Most of the time, they have lost most of the **$$$,** if not all of it. You say… how could they loose all of that? The Universe has a way of treating all of us. In order to have **$$$** and to keep **$$$**, you have to have a consciousness of wealth. Along with that consciousness of wealth is something called… I deserve this. You and I have to take hold of life that way. We have to do what we need to do every day so that at the end of the day we can reap the rewards. The rewards being a heart that feels satisfied… a job well-done. There is nothing that feels better than… job well-done. It's not something for nothing. As you give… so shall you receive. As you seek… so you find.

There are people who want spiritual enlightenment but they want it handed to them on a silver platter. They do not want to do the work that it takes to become enlightened. We can gain enlightenment from reading, listening and associating with enlightenment.

Doing the work is what solves the problem.
Winning the Lottery does not solve the problem.

#12 LIE... EXCUSE FOR FAILURE... THERE IS NO REASON TO STRIVE

One way to victimize people is to convince them that they are victims. You are not a victim. You have heard that before. That is a Unity teaching. In order for me to convince you that you are not, I will have to push some buttons.

You cannot use the excuse… well… that's just the way life is. NO. That is a lie. You can no longer do that. Once you decide to wake up and start to live… then you have to wake up and celebrate life. This is the truth. The minute that you decide to take control of your life… take the rein and do something about what has been bothering you… the Universe rushes in to give you some assistance. But… you have to take the rein… your have to step out there… and do it. Life is what you make it.

No one today knows how to live when everything is going well. What would you do if you had everything that you wanted? You would have to create something else that you wanted… to strive for. We think that having everything we want will bring us happiness… and it should. But… because we live in a world of when… not now… it doesn't bring us happiness. The minute we get everything we are striving for… we get bored.

If we are striving to live life to the fullest… we can. We keep ourselves from doing it so that we will have something to work for. If we use the power that is in us… if we say… God is my source… we are moving toward having the ability to achieve everything we want.

Let's say… we get it. Now what? Conventional religions talk about going to Heaven… sitting on the clouds… playing harps… singing in the Heavenly choir for eternity. The alternative was going to Hell and burning for eternity. Which is worse… eternal boredom…or burning in Hell?

We must strive for what we want. We just cannot accept life as it appears to be because we can change it. At the same time… we need to be happy with what we have. Sounds like a paradox… and it is. We need to do both. The more we learn about truth… we realize that each truth is a paradox. It is not either… or. It is both… and.

If I have everything that I want… I still have to get up and live life to the fullest. The minute that we give up… then life gives up on us. Often times people strive for retirement and when the reach it… when they no longer have anything to strive for… they curl up and die. They have nothing to get up for in the morning. If we tell ourselves that we have everything that we want… why get up? This attitude can even lead to suicide… the loss of will to achieve and to strive. How do we cure this? It is simple.

Do not let striving for earthly goods be your aim. Why? Because you can acquire that. The striving must be for spiritual maturity. There is enough to do there to last you out. That will see you through because we are striving to be the Christ. It takes several life- times to do that. If that is your goal… then you have work to do. It is not physical work. It is metaphysical work. You will always have a way to go. You will always have a reason to live. If you make our goal larger than life… you will never get bored.

Can your goal be to foster peace on earth? That is a little big. Can you foster peace in your household… peace among all of your friends? That is big enough to work on. Can it be… wherever I go… I bring peace?

A good mantra to live by might be:
I strive to bring higher consciousness everywhere I go.

That is a goal worth striving for.

#13 LIE... EXCUSE FOR FAILURE... PEOPLE CAN AFFECT MY SELF-ESTEEM

You can never help or hurt anyone's self-esteem. Have you ever used the lie… you have hurt my self-esteem? People say… the problem is… I don't have good self-esteem. Some people do have a problem with their self-esteem. That is usually at the bottom of everything that is going wrong in our life. However… it is never because of someone else. Therein lies the misconception. We think that it is someone else's problem… or that someone else can solve that problem. That is not the truth. When you think that some- one has not treated you well… and that it will affect your self-esteem… that is a lie. That may be difficult for you to accept.

Let's look at the word… self-esteem. It's what you think about yourself. How many times have I said… no one can affect me… but me. What you do is really about you… not about me. If someone wants to act like a jerk… that's them acting like a jerk. You say… they don't respect me. Well… they probably don't respect anybody. That is a reflection on them… not a reflection on you.

We have an idea about how we should be treated. If people don't do that… we get our feelings hurt. The point is… we spend so much time doing that… a waste of energy. We cannot control what other people do. Things do not change. People change. Things change only when our perception changes. When our attitude about it changes… it appears that the situation changes. Things are always a reflection of the way we think about them. If we change our thinking and our feeling… they appear to change… but… they don't. We have changed.

If we want to change our self-esteem… we have to change the way WE feel about our- selves. Someone who has high self-esteem in a certain area is unaffected by what other people might say about it. For example… if there is something that you do very well… and you know you do it well… if someone says… you don't do that very well… you just laugh at them. It does not push a button. When we get criticized in an area where we do not feel all that confident… then, they push the button. Then… we say… they make us feel that way. NO. It's because they reflected something that we feel about ourselves. It is always self-esteem.

Who has the power to raise or lower that self-esteem? Well... it's always an inside job. An event is simply an event until you and I respond to it. The minute we respond to it… we make it something that we take inside ourselves. Self-esteem is a result of our own opinion of our own thoughts and actions.

It's really about being true to yourself. How can I build self-esteem in certain areas which is related to the action that I take in that area? Actually… the action that I am willing to take is based on what I think. Actions are the only thing that can gather that inner-strength called self-esteem.

What does self-esteem really mean? It means thinking highly of yourself. For example… take an area in your life that you do not feel highly about. If you do what you know you need to do in that area… just by taking action in that area… you will build your self- esteem. You will be able to say… I am doing my part. When we begin to raise our self- esteem… it is always up to us. One can build self-esteem in a prison cell. It does not depend on the thoughts or actions of other people. Self-esteem is how we feel about our- selves. No one else has the power to change how you feel about yourself… unless… you don't have the fortitude to stand up for yourself.

We always want other people to do the work for us. I am the only one that can do the work for me in any area of my life. That is how I build self-esteem in any and all areas. How do I feel about me? Am I doing what I know I need to do in my life? That is a self- esteem builder.

If you start praising the actions of people… that is good to hear… but it does not raise their self-esteem. Parents think that all they have to do is praise their children and then their children won't have problems when they grow up. There is nothing wrong with praising kids. However… you don't want to praise them for doing nothing and you don't want to praise them for doing the wrong thing. Praising somebody when they know themselves that they are not doing it… does not raise their self-esteem. You say... kids need love and praise. Well… love and praise are two different things. I can love you without praising you. I can praise you without loving you. If you tell a child he is fantastic, and he does not think he is fantastic… he won't believe it. Hearing it does not make them feel that way about themselves unless they feel that way about themselves.

You can praise something they have done. By doing… we build our own self-esteem. If someone gets excited about doing something, and you say… that was really great that you did that… and the person knows that it was a great thing to do… they will feel good about that because you said something that is the truth. They know it to be the truth.

Self-esteem is about yourself. Suppose you are around some people and you are angry about the things they are saying… but… you don't say anything. That hurts your self- esteem. You are not standing up for what you believe. What we have not learned is… how to state an opinion without being obnoxious. Most people think that they need to get really mad and get confrontational instead of just calmly saying… you have the right to think that, but I disagree. That is a self-esteem builder.

Don’t fall into the lie that you can hurt my self-esteem. You cannot. You can remind me that I do not have high self-esteem in that area. But… you cannot hurt it. And… you can- not build it either.

Self-esteem lies within yourself.

#14 LIE... EXCUSE FOR FAILURE... OH, FOR THE GOOD OLD DAYS

Why does it seem when we look back on something that it was a lot better than it was? We look and we think… it was so good then. My mind has a way of erasing what was not right. I can color it the way that I want it to be. That is not exactly what holds us back. We have the right to color anything the way we want to… in the way we want to do it. But… if we get stuck in the past… we can't move forward.

I recently read a book about awakening to zero point. It has a lot of scientific information. It seems that the zero point to which they were referring was the magnetic field… the pull of the earth. They measured it. That dynamic pull of gravity is changing. What they found out was… people who had new ideas… who were progressive… who were not understood… lived in a place on the planet where there was less pull of gravity than other places. They realized that the places that had the most pull of gravity had people who were stuck in the past, and it was hard to get them to change.

That said… guess where there is less pull of gravity in the United States. Where do you think that was? It was along the West Coast. Can you understand why the rest of the country says that they tilted the United States, and all the nuts and bolts went to the West. It is because they don't understand us. There is less pull of gravity out here. Therefore… there is a lot more free-thinking here.

Guess where the greatest pull of gravity was. It was in the South. It is interesting to note that people in the South ancestor worship. They are the slowest people to change. They don't like change. They like to keep things exactly the way they are. The gravitational pull is much greater in the South than it is anywhere in the United States. The South has not made the progress that we make in the West. That is because they stay in the past. On the West Coast where the new things are being invented, and new ideas are being born… there is less tendency to live in the past and a greater tendency to live in the now.

So…when we tell ourselves… OH, FOR THE GOOD OLD DAYS… we are planting our feet in concrete. That is a lie that keeps us from progress of any kind. Every time you remember the way it was and you lie to yourself and tell yourself that was the good times… you are putting yourself in concrete. It is OK to look back and say… we had a good time. But… we really need to look at today. Today is the beginning of the rest of your life. So… let go of that past. Turn around and see what you can accomplish. Never say: "Well I couldn't do it then… so I certainly couldn't do it now." NO. Or… "I could have done it then because times were different. But…now I can't do it." NO. Life changes. When we talk about how bad life was… or how good life was… we are facing backward in life. It's the beginning of the end. Life is about forward movement.

The minute that we stop moving forward… we begin to die. Many people who retire, don't live very long. Some people retire and take up a whole new occupation. That is different.

There was a recent TV program that told about a company in Connecticut that the youngest employee was in his seventies. Some employees were in the nineties. These people had learned computers. They went to work every day… filled with enthusiasm. There was a set of stairs on the work site. The employer said… "as long as you can climb those stairs… you can work here." Those were the youngest ninety-year olds that I had ever seen. Why? Because they kept themselves young learning something new. These people were running a company that was keeping up with competitors that were staffed with young employees. The employer said that he found that his employees gave more and they were more loyal. He mentioned several reasons why they were exemplary employees.

These people did not say… "I can't. I give up. There is nothing left for me to do. My life is in the past." They did not go that way.

We are not to go that way. Your life is ahead of you. I don't care how old you are. You have a life ahead of you. Don't look back. Turn around. Let it go. Release and let go of the past. Above all… practice forgiveness. Don't hold grudges. They will hold you back. Move forward with your life. There are possibilities out there for you.

When we stay present to what can happen in our lives… then we open the door for it to happen. There is a brighter day for you today and tomorrow than you ever had in the past.

THE GOOD OLD DAYS ARE WAITING FOR YOU!

15 LIE...
EXCUSE FOR FAILURE...
THAT'S JUST THE WAY I AM

I can claim all kinds of characteristics and they can get me off the hook. But they are lies. I say… that's just the way I am… I can't remember anything… that's just the way I am… I am disorganized… that's just the way I am. If someone asks you to do something, you can get off the hook by saying…t hat just stresses me out… that's just the way I am. I like to keep a low profile… that's just the way I am. I'd love to help you, but I cannot sit in meetings… that's just the way I am. That is all self-defeat.

We are born with individual characteristics. We are each individuals, and we behave in an individual way. However… when we use these as an excuse… we are misusing them and we are telling ourselves lies. Each of us has within us a possibility to become a self- motivated person. We can make a decision to open up our Universe... to expand our- selves just a little bit. We don't have to stay the way we are. We can tweak it.

If someone takes on a responsibility and then backs out by saying… I can't really do it this way because that's not me… that's just the way I am. Well… it needs to be done that way in order for the project to succeed. We don't have to give up our individuality. We don't have to be just like everyone else. However… the Universe is always encouraging us to expand ourselves… to learn… to be flexible… to become something bigger.

Enlightenment means… to make yourself lighter. When we sell ourselves on… that's just the way I am… it keeps us locked into that fearful childhood. We can become heavy with a false claim of permanent personality… heavy with that lie. That is why enlightenment and growing up feel like the same thing. We were born to become enlightened. Each lie that we let go of… causes us to feel more enlightened in the process.

For example… do not say… 'I lost 25 pounds.' That implies that you need to find it. Instead… say… 'I released 25 pounds.' As you release your old idea of yourself… then you can release the protection. Excess weight is protection. We use these excuses for protection. When we throw aside those heavy lies that we are struggling to carry around with us… we can become free. That's growing up. It's growing lighter, and higher and free. Enlightenment is emergence from self-imposed immaturity.

If we didn't carry these lies around with us… then we would naturally grow up. You and I established a certain behavior when we were children and we had to face an adult challenge. Even parents have issues with which they have not dealt. So…

children growing up around them have to come up with their own idea of how to live. Those little quirks that we developed to get along in life… they served us very well. However… when we become an adult… we need to let go of those old things that we used to think about our- selves.

When you play poker, and someone asks you if you did well… you would not say… "NO…I was dealt a bad hand." If you played all evening… you were dealt many hands. That is the way it is with life. We are not dealt just one hand. However… we live like that. We live with the hand that we were dealt as children. We have defenses around that and then we decide… that's just the way we are. We don't realize that every day… we have been dealt a new hand of cards.

The clincher is… it's not the cards, anyway. It's how you play the cards. That's true with life. You can say… I have been dealt a bad hand in life. Maybe you were dealt one bad hand. However… you probably were dealt other good hands. You did not play those cards out because you were playing them as if they were a bad hand.

Life is something that evolves. We need to realize that. This will make you feel better about not having changed. Society does not like for us to change. Society does not give credence to the fact that people change and that people can change. People say… well... somebody changed them. That does not give credence to the fact that you and I can change on our own.

Don't go around saying:
"That's just the way I am."

Don't live that lie because it is a block that will keep you from growing.

Instead say: "That's the way I was. I used to be that way.
I am no longer that way."

Live the truth because it will allow you to celebrate life.

#16 LIE... EXCUSE FOR FAILURE... STRUGGLE MAKES ME STRONGER

Have you ever heard someone say… what doesn't kill me makes me stronger? What a lie that is. What that is telling us is that it's okay to say… I'm going to be stronger for having suffered. That is simply not the truth. Do you know people who are stronger from having suffered? That is a Piscean Age philosophy. That was the age of martyrdom. People lived with hair shirts and flogged themselves. There was something about suffering. Well… we have learned a lesson because we have moved out of that age and suffering is no longer in.

Now… think about that one thing that keeps happening to you that seems to be the anchor you are carrying around. We all have one. That anchor manifests itself in different ways and in different situations but it is really the same thing. What I've realized lately is that the situations in my life that I get upset about… is not really what I'm get- ting upset about. I know that sounds crazy, but underneath… there is a hook. If I can get rid of that hook… then the situations that seem to come up in every part of my life, that involve the same thing… will go away. Why? Because I won't have that hook any longer.

There are situations in life that bother us because we have a hook to attract them or a button to be pushed. We're talking about the same thing here… a hook and a button. The key is not to get rid of the situations that you and I are getting hooked on… not to get rid of the people that we are hooked on.

We need to get rid of the hook.
We need to get rid of the button.

You may think that letting go of our buttons… letting go of our hooks sounds easier said than done. That is not true. What has to happen before you can get rid of something is that you have to own that you have it. I have to own that I have a button there. I have to own that I have a hook there.The minute that I do that… then I can get rid of it.

Most of the time… you and I are pointing our fingers to those other people. We're saying… they are the problem… that situation always happens to me. They are the problem. The situation is the problem. It's not *my* fault. NO. That is not true. It always comes back to us. The situation is always me. The situation is always you. We cannot get around that.

We have to change our perspective and ask… what is this really about? What is it in me that is causing me to have this button? Not… why are they pushing my button? The question is… what is the button? I don't even have to go back to why I have the button. Just let me own that the button is mine. Let me own that the hook is mine. Let me take the energy off of *them* and put it on me.

John: 21:22 says…*What is this to me…come and follow me.* So… let us say… "What is this to me?" It is nothing. Let me follow the Christ in me. Let me look within and know that I am perfect in every way. Let me see the real me… the me that doesn't have a but- ton. The me that is perfect in every way because I Am the Christ. Under the buttons… under the hooks… under all of that stuff… is the perfection that you and I are seeking.

Don't say… what doesn't kill you makes you stronger. That is a lie. Let us say… what is the lesson here? That changes everything. Now I can see truth. You and I are here to grow and what that means is that we are to look inside ourselves and find out what we need to release.

We are talking about releasing the baggage that we are carrying around. We're talking about releasing the button… releasing the hook. You can never be hooked and no one can ever push your button if you don't have the hook and if you don't have the button.

Forget the struggle.
The struggle does not make you stronger.

#17 LIE... EXCUSE FOR FAILURE... I AM HELPLESS

This is a big one. This one goes straight to the soul… to the Sub-Conscious Mind. It is a mission to kill the spirit, to remove the passion and to deny our uniquely human power. This lie is created to convince ourselves that we have no power… that we are helpless. It just is not true. If you knew the truth about yourself… if you realized how absolutely powerful you were… you would make no excuses. You are not a victim. That is a difficult truth to understand.

In the book… Zero Point… it says that the Earth's magnetic pull is changing and that we want to resist doing anything about it. We want to feel helpless. We are not helpless. We need to watch. But… there is action that we can take. You are a powerful person. You have within you the power to create your own reality.

What we are doing now is living defensively. You allow things to happen out there and then you adjust your life accordingly. We do not need to live that way. We need to decide the direction and then create the flow the way we want it to go. Use that power. This is a dangerous spot. It sounds like I am saying that the Ego has the power to do that. That is not what I am saying. What I am saying is… the power within you is that Divine Power that flows through you. But… you have to connect with that power.

When Jesus said…*the Father and I are one*…when He said…*it is not I that does the work, it is the Father within*… he realized that it was the Divine Power within Him that was doing the work. So… we must be careful when we say… I am a powerful person. We are saying I AM a powerful person. God is the I AM. Moses asked God… what is your name. God replied. *I AM that I AM.* It is our I AM that is our Divine Power within us. So…whatever we call our I AM to…that has the power.

We use this power every day. We say… I AM good at that. We are linking that I AM with what we know to be the truth. The I AM has the power. In that way… you are *creating* reality rather than *responding* to reality.

If you are wanting to heal, or something you are wanting to do… you pull in that power. You connect your I AM with whatever it is you want to do. You say… I Am a powerful person. That is pulling that power that is in you into reality. You must be convinced that *the Father and I are one*… pertains to you. That the I AM power within you is one with you.

That internal Higher Power that you have access to… that is not your physical self… that is not your Ego… can become your physical self. But… it can only become your physical self if you consciously bring it into that part of you. Remember… it is not the Ego that is powerful. It is the Divine within you.

So…when you say… I AM helpless… you are putting your I AM into helpless. You don't ever want to say that. I assure you that it does not matter what the situation is… it does not matter who you are up against… you can use this power to come up with a reality that you never dreamed possible and put it into play. You are never helpless as long as you connect with the I AM power that is in you. Those are powerful words. You are never helpless. Don't ever tell yourself that lie.

You are a powerful person. You may not have accessed that power, but… it is there. A dam has water behind it. The dam has the ability to make electricity. If the water is not let out of the dam… that does not mean that it cannot be let out. You look at the dam and you look at the water. The water is not going out and you say… this does not have any power. It does not have power until you put it to work. The potential is there.

We have dammed up the power within ourselves.
We need to let it out by saying… I AM a powerful person.
Where is that power coming from?
It is coming from our Higher Self.
Let's put our power to work.

YOU ARE NEVER HELPLESS

CHAPTER THREE
THE 12 POWERS

We have been given 12 powers. The 12 powers are gates that open into the Kingdom of Heaven... the Holy City Within. These gates are 12 parts of our mind... Divine ideas. When we are locked outside of the Kingdom, we can enter by any one of these gates. These are the gifts that we have been given to celebrate life. We go and hangout at a particular gate… we go where we need empowering. These are powers that we need to learn how to use. To receive the power that you have always looked for, you have to go within… go within and hang out with God.

The 12 faculties of our mind are the 12 potential powers of our mind. We develop faculties into powers. We have to cultivate a faculty just as if it were a seed. You plant the seed. However... if you let weeds grow up around it, and if you don't cultivate around it, it doesn't have a chance to grow into maturity. We now acknowledge that we have these seeds of these powers and through cultivation, they will grow into powers:

FAITH

IMAGINATION

LAW AND ORDER

LIFE

LOVE

POWER

RENUNCIATION

STRENGTH

UNDERSTANDING

WILL

WISDOM

ZEAL

FAITH

I have Faith in the Universal Power in me.

Faith is the substance of things hoped for...
the evidence of things not seen.
Faith is the perceiving power of the mind
linked with the power to shape substance.

Whatever you have faith in, that is the perceiving of the mind. The perceiving power of the mind is something that you already have. You perceive life to be a certain way. You perceive yourself to be a certain way. You link that with the power that shapes substance. Substance is God stuff. It is invisible... you can't see it... you can't smell it. But... it is everywhere present. It is all around you. The perceiving power of the mind... when you link it with substance, it shapes it. Faith is the key. We all have perceiving powers of the mind. We know that there is substance, but, Faith is the thing that shapes it. It is the spiritual assurance that we can create our reality.

Think about Faith for a minute. We all have Faith. It is not about acquiring more Faith. It is about cultivating Faith in God... the Universal Power in me. Cultivate that Faith and life turns around.

If you are holding a heavy book, and you are standing up, you know that if you release that book, it will fall to the floor. What do you have Faith in? You have Faith in gravity. We all have Faith, but we need to have faith in the right thing, because we are already linking our mind to the ability to shape substance. We are creating the reality that we live in. You created your reality whether you believe it or not.

We always create everything we have in our lives. That is our ability to shape substance. Shaping substance then becomes our reality. Whatever we have Faith in, that is shaped from substance and then appears in our lives is our reality.

The trick here is to do this consciously... to know that you have the power. Faith in the reality of things spiritual, is the Faith that we need in our mind. When the mind is filled with this Faith, it creates this halo that we have heard about. You have seen pictures of the saints, and they all have a halo around their heads... that is because they had total Faith in God. They had a highly developed spiritual Faith.

I have more Faith in my Spiritual-Self than I do in my ego-self. I have total Faith in my Spiritual-Self. Left on my own without the spiritual Faith, I would be left without the God power that is in me. **It is the Father Within that does the work**. If you have some- thing that you want to accomplish... whether it's prosperity...

whether it's health... whether it's love... the way you get it is through spiritual Faith. That is where you get the power.

The power comes in the Faith that God will supply. Left to my own devices, I know that I cannot create it. I know that God can create it. However... I need the spiritual Faith to know that God can create it through me. That's the trick... by the power that is me... God in me.

Do you have Faith that you speak the word and it is done? If you say... No... then what you are relying on is your ego-self... not your Spiritual-Self. Do you have Faith in your Spiritual-Self? Can you go within and connect with that part of you that makes you feel whole and perfect in every way? Speak the word and know that it will happen? That's Faith. That's Faith in the way it was created to be. My Faith is in the power in me through God. That is the Faith that we are talking about... spiritual Faith. You don't have to be a minister to do this. This is a power that is in me... a power that is in you. I have Faith in the Universal Power in me.

Faith is the substance of things hoped for...
the evidence of things not seen.

The assurance of things hoped for. Doesn't that mean that I know that when I speak the word that things that I hoped for will manifest? Yes... that is the power we have.

I have Faith in the Universal Power in me.

IMAGINATION

Intuition and Imagination are the Gold Dust Twins

Intuition: God's call… no negotiation… the truth… Divine inspiration... infallible… a hunch

Imagination: Your call… unlimited mental picturing… can be positive or negative

Imagination is more important than knowledge.
~ Albert Einstein ~

We all present to the world our own idea of who we think we are. Whatever it is you think of yourself… that's what you present to the world. Other people probably have a better idea of who you think you are than you do.

What would you like for other people to think of you? You need to be whatever that is in your imagination… a new image of yourself. When you look in the mirror and you see everything about you that you don't like… that's what you concentrate on. Many people don't like the way they look. If you focus on the part of yourself that you don't like… that part just gets bigger for some reason. Everybody has good points. There must be something about yourself that you like. Focus on that. Let that get bigger. Let that be the part that you notice. Your Sub-Conscious Mind does not know the difference between factuality and imagination. As you begin to concentrate on what you want… how you want to look… see yourself looking that way. You will begin to look that way. You will. The imagination is how to get there.

Imagination is the scissors of the mind. It is like cutting pictures so that you can be that. The minute that you hook up your imagination with your feelings… you begin to build that into your world. We build our imagination by using it. Practice… Practice… Practice. We need to start using this faculty that we have. This is a God-given gift. When we study truth… we learn that this is how we create our reality. Life is always the way you think it's going to be. That's the way it is. People can go through the same experience. Some will look at it as terrible. Some will look it as OK. Some will look at it as fabulous. It can't be all of those things. Yet… it is. Your experience of it is your definition that you use for it.

We create our reality. We create what we have in our lives. Imagination is the faculty of the mind that images and forms. Think of imagination as imaging. Everything that is manifested in this world and in your world was first a mental picture. When we form those mental pictures, we are bringing into reality the forming power of our lives. What you can see yourself doing… that's your reality. If you cannot see yourself doing it… then that's your reality. The imaging power of the mind… that 's what our imagination is. The imagination molds and shapes substance into form.

The thought you have is a mold. It is the form into which you pour substance. That thought is an image. When we think in words or pictures… that thought is an anticipation of what might happen. You are imagining it. There is so much power in that. We don't think about it. Someone who has a vivid imagination, has the ability to create in a magnificent way... to create out of the box.

When we go to the movies… those pictures we see on the screen were first an idea. They were then moved into words that became pictures that were then translated by people acting out the picture of the words. You and I look at it on the screen and we become all emotional. We sometime laugh… or cry… at these images on a flat screen. Nobody is up there. But… there is a picture and we believe it. We are convinced. By the same token… what goes on in your mind is very convincing to you. You can play it out. You can invent the rest of the movie.

Let's say… an incident happens at work. Your boss looks at you funny. You get the feeling that something is not right. Then… the mind goes to work. The mind then begins to play out what might happen, and in your imagination, you create a scenario. If you dwell on that scenario long enough… you are literally creating the end of the story. The imagination forms the reality.

Can you imagine a different ending? Go back and say… that was really a smile. Then you picture out a scenario with a happy ending. Make your own movie. Make it to your liking. When you do that… what begins to happen is you begin to form a reality that can actually take place. Make your own movie. We do that, anyway. We are the writers We are the directors. We are the producers. We are the actors.

What kind of movie are you making to live out as your reality? That is the power of your imagination. The imagination fixed on Holy Spirit creates a reality of perfection. With our imaginations, we can hold to perfect ideas and then clothe them in substance. No one controls your thinking. No one can control your mind.

Suppose you write a script in which you are a character who is a winner… who is happy… who is healthy… who is prosperous beyond imagination. See yourself that way… play it out in your mind and keep on playing it out until it materializes for you.

There is flip side of the coin. A worst-case scenario played out in our heads is where we usually stay most of the time. Prepare for the worst... hope for the best. Prepare for the worst. Can you see where that phrase, alone, can lead you down the garden path to destruction? If you are preparing for something to happen… believe me… it's going to happen. If you play it out in your mind… get ready. That's exactly what's going to hap- pen.

Suppose you want to be able to write well. You need to think of yourself as writing well. The first thing is… you begin to write. You may not be all that good at first. You may be able to think it, but putting it down on paper may be another matter. You know that your thoughts are good. You know that there is no reason that you cannot do it. So… tell your- self to do it. If your thoughts are good… the writing is going to be good. You will grow into it. Open up your intuition to give you a new idea and then use your imagination to picture yourself as writing well. Imagine someone being grateful to publish your work. Before you know it… you'll have a book written and it will be a big success. You may think this to be a big undertaking. However… a book is written one word at a time… a page at a time. It is easy once you get into it.

You have to open yourself up to new ideas. If you want a change in your life… you can- not continue to do things the way you have always done them. You have to open up your imagination. The positive use of your imagination will be great mental and spiritual training. It's fun. Whatever you imagine with feeling is how you build it into your life. When you begin to imagine things that you would like to have come into your life… they will begin to do that because your Sub-Conscious Mind does not know the difference between fantasy and actuality. You need to imagine things in your life as having been done… NOW. Imagine them in every detail. The more vivid and the more detailed they are… the sooner they are going to happen.

As you do this… ask God to give you more and more imaginings… to make you a whole new being through the use of your imagination… to improve everything in your world. As you begin to improve everything in your world… you will begin to improve the world around you. If you envision yourself as living peacefully… having peace of mind… it will flow over to other people. When your cup runneth over… it flows over to others. Your imagination is your gift from God. If you can imagine it… you can have it.

You and I are led by the media today into constant fear. Why? Because we have 24-hour television. The time has to be filled, and good news doesn't sell. We are only interested in worst-case scenarios. We are only interested in those terrible things that happen to *other* people. We have probably thought about all those things and when we can see them happening to someone else, it makes us feel a little safer. If it happens to *them*… then it won't happen to *me*. It got *them* instead of *me*. That causes us to continue to feed on that path of imagining the worst. The media feeds it to us because they know we will watch it.

Why do they want this audience? Audiences sell ratings. Ratings run the show. If you had a network that just had good news… it would be off the air very soon. Nobody would watch it. The NEWS stations not only give us the bad news… they run a little strip along the bottom of the screen showing dire devastation events because there is more bad news than they can show at one time. Those little strips never tell any good news.

In ***The Wizard of Oz***...the Wicked Witch of the West said: *Don't nobody bring* me *no bad news.* She knew exactly what she was saying. She had it right. Don't tell me those horrible things that could happen. I don't want to hear it. If I get it in my head... I will create it.

All this fear is playing on our imagination. If you want a perfect world... you have to imagine it first. If you want that perfect job... you have to see yourself in the job. You have to imagine the office... you have to see your desk. You have to see yourself looking the way you want to look doing that job. See yourself in that position. Hold that image in your mind until it manifests as your reality. Don't play that worst-case scenario.

People talk about saving for a rainy day. I'm not against saving. But I do not agree with that slogan. Turn your savings account into a fun account. Have the money there for a fun event. Don't save for the rainy day. If you save for a rainy day... you are going to get a rainy day. It is in your mind, and you are imagining it every time you put that money in. Every time you put the money in... imagine it is for a fun event and you'll have enough money for everything.

You and I create our reality. How are you imagining yourself to be? We build into our consciousness what we want to happen and we do that by using the faculty of imagination. To make it stick... what you imagine can become your new way of thinking if the desired images are imbedded into your Sub-Conscious Mind. To accomplish this... the Conscious Mind get out of the way and the Sub-Conscious Mind must be brought for- ward. This can be accomplished through Self-hypnosis. In this altered state of consciousness... which is similar to meditation... the Sub-Conscious Mind is now ready to receive the positive, powerful suggestions you wish to program into it. This technique can be used successfully to accomplish any goal you set for yourself: Smoking Abolishment, Weight Management, Monetary Success... to name a few.

The Sub-Conscious Mind will believe anything you tell it. It cannot tell the difference between fact and fiction. I saw a demonstration of a person who was in the hypnotic state being told that her arm was going to be touched by a lighted cigarette. She was actually touched by a pencil. A blister came up on her arm. It was not burned. It was touched by a pencil. She was told under hypnosis that she had been burned. The body reacted. The blister came up.

When the Sub-Conscious Mind thinks something is happening... it makes it happen. The Sub-Conscious Mind does not think. It obeys. We must get into our Sub-Conscious Mind the way we want our life to be. Then... that is the way it will be. We do that by using our imagination. We fake it till we make it. We play-like it has already happened. Kids do play-like all the time. That is a perfect way of developing imagination. Too bad we have been taught that we must out-grow out child-like fantasies. We are told that we must grow up. Jesus said…*ye must become as little children.* He was referring to that child-like quality of imagination. He knew exactly what He was talking about.

You and I can use the faculty of imagination to create what we want. What do you want in your life? Have you ever just sat down and decided what you want? What do you want in a relationship? What are your dreams? What are your goals? When you identify all that… then, you imagine that it's done. See yourself doing it. You play-like it is happening. The next thing you know… it is happening.

What idea do you have about human relations? What idea do you have about your sup- ply? What idea do you have about your health? You may not like it… once you have faced it. You may not like the picture you have of yourself. Thank God… you can change it. That is our prerogative.

As a truth student… it is your mission to present God's image and likeness of the Son of God to the world. Truth means the laws of the Universe… which means God. We are children of God. We are made in the image and the likeness of God. We are to present that image to the world. We are to present God's image and likeness for our body. For that part of our body that may not be functioning well… we have to picture it functioning perfectly. The perfect function for you and me is to function perfectly. Jesus said… *I must be about my Father's business.* What is the Father's business? It is to present in a perfect way. Jesus also said… *be ye perfect as your Father in heaven is perfect.* Where is the Father in heaven? It is inside of us… Jesus called it… *the Father Within.*

Most people don't even know what they want. They are so busy playing catch-up. We have to stop living in defense of what is happening around us and begin to state what we want to happen. One of my favorite verses is: *What is this to me?* Turn a deaf ear to what is happening around you. Turn your back on it. That is what Jesus meant when he said: *Get thee behind me Satan.* He was referring to wrong-minded thinking. Turn your back on it. Walk away from it. *What is this to me?* I am busy creating a reality to my liking.

Some people cannot imagine beyond their current limited thinking. You have to stretch. You stretch a little bit at a time. Before you know it… you have gone further than you ever thought possible. Stretch a little bit at a time. Always imagine your highest and best. Never go second class. Always travel first class in your mind, and that is what you will experience in your life. Imagination is always traveling first class.

You can intuit things. That comes from God. That is God speaking to you through your intuition. Then… use your imagination to build on it. Only you can develop that gift. Most people have developed their imagination to their detriment. They imagine all of the negative things that could happen. Most people can tell you what might happen… bad. They are using their imagination, but… they are using it in the wrong way. They are using Murphy's Law. Don't even go there. *If anything can go wrong... it will.* Don't even go there. Declare and decree that life is good. Life is fabulous. And it is.

Wake up to the possibility of what you can do...
not what you can't do and your life will be great.

It is so simple.

You just need to tweak the way that you are thinking.
Remember… your imagination creates your reality.

My imagination creates my reality.

Be careful what you imagine… you might just get it.

LAW AND ORDER

I declare Divine Order in my life.

Life is such a fabulous thing. It doesn't matter what is going on in the world. What matters is our perception of it. People miss that all the time. There are different interpretations of what we see going on around us. We interpret it according to who we are and that becomes our truth. I am speaking of our relative truth. On the other hand… Absolute Truth is totally unchangeable. Our relative truth is changeable.

Absolute Truth is what I am talking about when I am talking about God. God is Universal Energy and it never changes. It is what it is. You can depend on that. If you and I place all of our eggs in that basket of relative truth… they are destined to get broken because it changes constantly. That relative truth is our perception. If we are growing at all… our perception changes. What we thought we could count on… we can't count on. But… we can always count on Absolute Truth. We can always count on God. We can always count on the laws of God… the laws of the Universe.

In Unity, law and order are more frequently referred to as Divine Order. However… law is order because the first law of the Universe is order. We talk about balance… in every- thing there is balance. Everything is in order. When you have everything in balance, then you have everything in harmony.

THE LAWS OF THE UNIVERSE
Like attracts like.
Like begets like.
Thoughts become things.

CAUSE and EFFECT
What goes around comes around.

As you do unto others, it will be done unto you. Does that mean that others will do it? No… the law does it. The law is the logical process by which the Divine Principle…God…manifests. God manifest through this law because it is order. It is the way that Jesus taught and lived His life… Divine Order.

I declare Divine Order in my life.

If you do that… what are you declaring? You are calling in harmony. You are calling in balance. You are calling the Universe to come and straighten it out.

You and I do not make the law. The law is. It was established for our benefit long before the world was formed. The law is spiritual and mental growth and is constantly at work in the mind… raising us from one consciousness to another. As we linger in the Christ Consciousness, or Divine Order, we align ourselves with the laws of the Universe. The minute we are aligned… like attracts like. We are calling it in.

Let's think about the law. This is something that runs the Universe. Divine Law… Divine Order is God manifested on the planet. The law is God. God is order. As you and I align ourselves with this… we align ourselves for our greatest good.

You and I have the idea that we know how to run our lives. There is nothing wrong with that, except… we run our lives according to what we know… what the ego knows to be right and wrong. Well… we don't know everything. A Course In Miracles says: *What I know is not all there is to know.* Therefore… how could I possibly make the right decision if I don't know the facts? I know what I know. But… why not call in Divine Order? Why not turn it over to law and order? Why not get the information that I need and ask for Guidance? As I form my thoughts, that will become my reality.

LAW

Let's talk law and then we will go into order. What you think… you create. If you think fear… you get fear. You are pulling it into yourself. You are attracting it. In the Old Testament, Job said… *My fears have come upon me.* Of course. Don't we usually dwell on what we are afraid of? We call that preparing, but it's not… it's simply drawing it to us because like attracts like. Like begets like. We are planting that seed thought into the Universe so that it grows and multiplies. One tomato seed multiplies into 100 tomatoes. You not only get the same thing back… you get it in abundance. We live in a Universe of prosperity and abundance. You plant something you really want and it comes back 100 fold. Thoughts become things. What you dwell on… manifests in your life. What you put your attention to… manifests in your life. The law works.

ORDER

There is order in this Universe. That is the first law of the Universe. That is the reason you can count on it. When you plant a garden, you know that whatever seed you plant, that is what you are going to get. If you plant green bean seeds, you would not expect to get rutabagas. That's Divine Order. You can count on it. What you plant is what you get. That is the order that we live in. This is a power that we have… a power to call in order… a power to use the law for our benefit. We know that if we plant seeds of joy… seeds of prosperity… seeds of health… seeds of joy, seeds of prosperity and seeds of health what we plant will come up. The seeds come from our thoughts. We speak and that is planting the seed. We think and that is planting the seed. This is the order in which we live. It is perfect order.

I declare Divine Order in my life.

LIFE

The energy of infused and in quickened life is active in me now.

Did you ever think about life as being a power? Well… it is. We need to wake up to this power that is in us. Life is really a phase of being. It is the expression that manifests as animation, activity and vigor. Just breathing… that is not life. Life is something that hap- pens with or without a body.

You and I mostly identify life that is in a body. We don't have any trouble identifying that. But… when the body is gone… we think that life is gone. No. Life is everlasting. Life is eternal. God is life. You cannot kill God. You cannot kill life. Life that takes up residence in a body doesn't die when that body dies. The consciousness of eternal life places one in a stream of life that never fails. We need to be conscious of that.

One of the things that born-again Christian ministers teach is that when you are saved that you have eternal life, and when you are not saved… you are damned and go to hell. Well… if you don't have eternal life in hell… then you are not going to get that awful punishment they say you are going to go to hell to get punished for. So… you have eternal life either way. Unity and A Course In Miracles do not teach that there is a hell.

What is time? Time is really irrelevant when you get on the other side of the veil. Now... right now… is a moment in eternity. Eternity goes backwards as well as forward. It does not start now and go forward. It always is… always was… always will be. The only point in time that you and I have to express to the fullest… is now. I can't express in the past. I can't express in the future. I can only express… now.

As I think intently about life, it quickens it into action. When we talk about energy and force and power and life, we make those life currents flow through us throughout our whole being. Every time we talk about it, they hear that. Did you know that your body and energy hear you? It's kinda' like when E. F. Hutton speaks… everyone listens. When we speak, every thing of us listens and obeys. That's the power that we have. As you and I speak… the body listens… the energy that is in the body listens.

So… as we affirm that I am filled with life energy that is active and full of zeal, my body says… OK. Let's activate that power. That's how it works. During our higher realizations of truth, we are often conscious of this abiding flame that is working through us. Think of life as a flame. Think about it as you are reading these pages… reading these truths… that all the cells of our organisms are infusing this into Christ Consciousness and causing healing. We are infusing the words into our physicality.

This is what we call the new birth… being born again. That is transforming our body by raising it to electrical energy. We are raising the energy of our body. The next step in Divine evolution is the spiritualization of the body. This is done by bringing the most life... Divine Life...into our body. When I say bringing it into it... I mean infuse it so that our bodies become Divine.

We know our spiritual part is already Divine. We have bodies to clothe them so that we can live on this earth. When we no longer live on this earth, we still have the spiritual body, but we don't have the physical body. Our job is to bring spirit into physicality. We are to spiritualize the body.

I am going to go out on a limb, here...as if I have not already. Now don't just fall out when I say this. We are here to live in eternity in these physical bodies. We are working on it. Granted... we have not gotten there yet. Although... there are some people who are living in India that are 300 years old. They are getting there.

You and I as we spiritualize the body with life... we fill the cells. Our spiritual self already has eternal life. As we spiritualize the body... we are infusing the body with life... eternal life. Let's say our affirmation again:

The energy of infused and in quickened life is active in me now.

The energy of a quickened life is active in me now. Now that we know more than we did when we said it the first time... let's move it a little bit.

The energy of a quickened life is active in my body now.
My body is sizzling with life.

This is celebrating life. It's waking up to the possibility. It's waking up to something that we have not had before. This is really what we are talking about. This is the power of life... infusing the body with the power of life.

Sometimes when we feel tired, and we feel HO-HUM... it's not because the spiritual body is not infused with the activity of life... it is because the physical body is not. So... as we speak these words of truth... my body is infused with vital life and all its components are working in Divine harmony. That is what activates us.

We want to feel fabulous. We want to have health. Active life is whole and well. It is not ill. It is health personified. A vital life is prosperous. Vital life is filled with love. As we call this energy into our body, we are furthering evolution as we appear younger. We live longer. We live the life we were meant to live. We celebrate the power of life.

LOVE

Love is the only answer.

These 12 powers are powers that are in every one of us. They are gifts that we have that we can use for living life more fully. This lesson is talking about the power of love. Whenever there is a question… love is the answer. Love is a Divine Energy. That love is the highest energy of the Universe. That is why we can say… God is Love. God is always the answer. Universal energy of togetherness is always the answer. Love is what holds the Universe together. It is the glue of the Universe. Love is the fulfillment of the law.

The Greeks describe 4 kinds of Love:
Storge… Affectionate Love
Eros… Romantic Love
Philos… Brotherly Love
Agape… Unconditional Love
The Love that we are discussing is Agape.

This Universe that we live in is all energy. But… there are different degrees of energy. Let's review the laws of the Universe:

Like attracts like.
Like begets like.
Thoughts become things.

Love attracts love. If love is the highest energy, then it has the ability to pull things up to its level. Let's assume you are having a conflict with someone. What's the answer to the conflict? Is the answer to fight back… blow by blow… seeing who can hit the hardest? Now… someone is really mad. You lose a friend. However… if you pour love into the situation, you heal the situation because love is the universal healer. Love is the universal empowerer. Love is universal harmony. Pour love energetically into the situation and allow love to do the work. In the Book of John it says…*God is love.* So…we can say we are pouring God into the situation. God is the universal healer. Love and God are interchangeable.

Let's get back to like attracts like. When I am sending you bad energy, that opens the door for you to send it back. Like begets like. What you give birth to produces more just like it. If I send you less than love energy, I have opened the door for that energy to come back to me and I get to receive what I send.

Now… I have no control over you… whatsoever. That is of no consequence to me because I am only going to receive what I send. So… you can do anything to me that you want to do. You have simply opened the door for it to come back to you. No matter what you give me… I give you love. What am I going to get back… love. If you are sending me less than love… and I am sending you love… we are each attracting what we are sending. Suppose someone is accusing you of doing something, and you say… I did not do that. No… you did not do that … they did that. They are simply receiving what they sent and accusing you of doing it.

Love is the great harmonizer. Love is a builder. It restores. It reconstructs. That is what God is. God restores the world. Goodness everlasting and joy beyond expression… that's what love is. It is a willingness and a seeking on my part. I send love in every situation. Love is the only answer… the only answer for me. It's the only answer for you. As I send love, I receive love.

Now… isn't that the answer to the law? Isn't that the fulfillment of the law? What is it that we want in our world today? We want the end of karma. You and I have to play out what we give out. That's the way the law works. In other societies… that's called karma. So… how do I get off of the wheel of karma? What's the answer? I cannot do anything about the past. What I gave out is going to come back to me. That's the way it works. How do I stop the process? This is how you do it.

Whatever happens to you… it is a payback for something that you did in the past. If it's good… it's a payback for something good you did. If it's not so good… that's the way it. The Universe is not paying you back. No… you are paying you back. What goes around… comes around. If you want to get off that wheel of karma, what do you do? You send love… in every situation. This is a power. It is a power to get ourselves out of bad situations today, all future bad situations. Whatever happens… you send love. That way… whatever comes back to you is always love. You can control that. That is the power of love.

If everything in your life is in harmony… everything in you life is in love. Everything in your life is in God. Love is the harmony of the Universe.

Love is the answer to every question.

When I talk about sending love to someone who is not being very kind to you… what does that look like? We have the intention… the willingness of sending them well- being… harmony. We sent them… I wish you well. I wish harmony in your life. I wish healing in your life. I have no bad feeling to you.

Now… you understand… I don't have to like you. I don't have to want to be around you. But… I send you love. I hope that everything works out for you. I hope you are healed. I send you light. The light of God is the love of God. I send you God.

Love is the great overcomer. It overcomes hate… resistance… opposition… anger… and jealousy. Love is the great healer. God is love.

BE FILLED WITH THE POWER OF LOVE.

POWER

Through the Holy Spirit, I am powerful.

I hope you have decided that life is going to be good for you right now. Are you aware that you cannot control what other people do, or say, or think? There is no point in even trying. The only people we have control over is ourselves. We can control what we think. We do have power over ourselves. Let's begin to execute that instead of going out and trying to convert others to our way of thinking.

Right now, we are going to talk about power. That is one of our 12 powers. It is one of the faculties that grows into a power. Remember the old steam engines on the railroad? They would start very slow. Then they would build up speed as they built up steam. That slow movement was the power that it took to start that train into moving. It was immense, and was a lot more than it took to keep it running. Once it got running, it did not take as much power.

When we think about power, let's think about the ability to get things started. Power was represented by the disciple, Philip. In Greek, Philip means horsepower. Our Affirmation:

Through the Holy Spirit, I am powerful.

All of us have a certain amount of power… a faculty born in us. Remember… faculties develop into powers. That development comes from the Holy Spirit. The bible says… *Yeshall receive power when the Holy Spirit comes upon you.* Are you open and receptive to the Holy Spirit? The Holy Spirit is known as the activity of God. Father, Son and Holy Spirit. What we have here is that we allow the activity of God to be in us, and that brings forth our power.

You and I are meant to be the power of God in action. That's who we were meant to be. We have the power to control our thinking. That is probably the highest gift that we could ever have. Our thinking is the universal creative force for you and for me. I hold my thoughts… God fills them with God substance… and that's how I create my life. What- ever I think is my reality. That is why you cannot go changing other people. They have created a reality according to the way they think… just as you and I do. They have to first change their thinking in order to change their reality… just as you and I do. What greater power could there be than for you and me to be able to control what world we live in.

Each of us lives in a different Universe. Have you ever been somewhere with someone, and they start relating back to you what happened, and you say… that's not what happened. In their mind… that's what happened. It's their truth. In your

mind… something else happened… and that's your truth. Which one of you is right? You're both right. The Universe that you live in is your very own. You see it the way it is to you. This power comes into effect when you realize that you have the power to control your thinking.
So… let's call in Holy Spirit, and let's call in Divine Order and let us pronounce the world good. Let the prayer be… let me see life as a gift of God. Life is love, beauty, and perfection. What am I doing here? I am using the power of my words. The power to change formless into form comes from the vibration of my words.

Through the Holy Spirit, I am powerful.

I have the power to control my thinking. I have the power to change the world that I live in simply by changing the way that I think about it. The Bible says… *all power is given unto me in heaven and in earth*. Heaven is the mind where we form. Heaven is the total perfection. We can think in the idea of perfection… then we can speak those words. The power is that those words come into expression in our lives. We are able to experience that perfection. Here is a quote from *The True Lent* by Charles Fillmore:

All the issues of my life are stirred into action by the quickening Christ power, and I have dominion over my thoughts and feelings.

That is the power that is in us. The world that you and I live in is a world of our own creating. We have that power. We create this private Universe that we live in. We create our heaven and our hell by the way we think… by the way we perceive life to be. It is in your power to change. It is in your see life differently. This power is one of our faculties to be developed into a power. It is in our throat. It is in the power of the voice.

What do you say everyday? Do you speak your doom into existence? Do you say… "I will never understand this?" Do you say… "this test is going to be hard?" You are creating the difficulty. Say with all of your heart… "It's a piece of cake. Life is great. I feel fabulous." When I do this… I am sending a vibration into the Universe, and the Universe must send me back exactly what I send out. As I give… so do I receive. That is the power that we have.

Through the Holy Spirit, I am powerful.

RENUNCIATION

I release and I let go.

Renunciation is also called elimination and it is one of my favorite powers. It is important because before we can go through a process of growth, we have to get rid of the old stuff. I love the word... stuff. When you go on a trip... you can travel light, or you can pack all your stuff. What happens when you pack all your stuff? You have it with you, but it is burdensome. It is tiring to carry around. I used to be a heavy packer when I traveled. Then... I realized... I don't need all this stuff that I am carrying around every day.

That's the way it is with life. This stuff that you are carrying around... this old stuff... is holding you back. There is no such thing as new stuff. It is not stuff until it gets old. You and I are constantly acquiring... both in real life and in metaphysical life. But... you have to get rid of the old stuff to make room for the new experiences you want to acquire. It's not that you are going to quit acquiring. NO. That's life. That would be like saying... I don't need to eliminate any more because I am not going to eat any more. You have to eat to live. You also have to eliminate to live. There is a power called the power of renunciation.

That is the power where forgiveness comes into play. The stuff that you and I are carrying around are things that we have not wanted to let go of... old hurts... old things that we like to re-live every now and then... old stuff that we drag out when we want to feel sorry for ourselves. We need to forgive... and forget. People say... I can forgive... but I'll never forget. If you still have issues with it... you have not forgiven.

People freak out when we start talking about forgiveness because people do not under- stand what forgiveness is. When you forgive someone, it doesn't mean that it's OK. People think that when you forgive them you are saying that what they did was all right... lets make up and be friends. It was OK... do it to me again. I forgive you. That's not what forgiveness is at all. Forgiveness is that you will no longer let that occupy space in your thinking.

Let's assume that I perceive that someone did something to me 5 years ago, and I am still irritated by that. In fact... every now and then it just comes up and I chew on it like a cow chews on its cud. We belch it up and chew on it. That's what we do when we haven't forgiven someone. We bring it up again and again and re-live it. We get mad all over again. It's like it just happened and we get furious about it. Now... this is something that someone did to me five years ago. Do you think they remember that? No. Do you think that they are bringing it up every so often and re-living it and are furious. NO. They probably are just living their lives, and having a good time. That makes us even madder. We are fuming with this and they don't even care. The point is… they are through with it. They probably don't even know they did it. Who is this hurting that we are not forgiving? It's hurting us. Why is it hurting us? Because thoughts held in mind, create after their kind. You are holding on to bitterness. You are holding on to anger. Those are the emotions that hurt us. Those are the emotions that cause heart attacks. We think that it's hurting the other person… but… it's not. It's hurting us.

So… when we forgive, it means that we release it or we eliminate it from our lives. You're not saying… it's OK. Do it to me again. No. It's not OK, but no longer let that take up room in my consciousness. We can release it and let it go. Don't let what some- one else has done to you continue to hurt you. That means that they continue to have power over you even though they are not anywhere around you. That's giving them this power. NO. Let it go. Don't let it harm you over and over and over. Every time we re-live something from the past that harmed us, it does it all over again. That's why we need to forgive and release. Release them to their highest good.

This is how *A Course In Miracles* tells us how to accomplish forgiveness.
It is a 3-step process.

Step One: Identify the problem. Remember, we said that if we try to forget or deny the problem, we will just keep recalling it. So… don't deny that the event happened. Acknowledge it.

Step Two: Let it go. Just say… it happened… so what? I have no investment in allowing this to affect me. If you cannot let it go all at once…be willing to let it go. If you can't be willing… be willing to be willing.

Step Three: Call in the Holy Spirit to finish what you were unable to do. This will complete the willingness to let it go. These 3 steps are identical to the first 3 steps of the AA 12-Step Program.

When you are unforgiving, you are holding the other person prisoner. They are in the prison of your hate and anxiety. If someone is in prison, the jailer has to be there to make sure they are there. If you are the jailer, you are saying… OK… are you still there? Let me see…let me remember that I don't like you. Let me remember every detail of what you did to me. Well… when the jailer lets the prisoner go… the jailer gets to go home, too.

The law is truth. And truth is that all is good. There is no power and no reality in what we call sin. If sin were real and enduring… like goodness and truth… then it could not be forgiven. It would always be there. It would always hold its victim. As we enter into an understanding of the real and the unreal… a light dawns on us and we begin to see what Jesus meant when he said: *The son of man has the power on earth to forgive sin.* Who is the son of man? You and I. We are the *son of man*. We are Divine sparks. That's who we are. We have the power to forgive sin.

It is important that we understand the meaning of the word *sin*. When the Bible was being translated into English during the Elizabethan era… it had gone through several translations already… Aramaic… Greek… Latin. What they were looking for was one word that meant missing the mark… not getting it right. They had a word that just fit that. It was an archery term. During the Elizabethan era… they shot bows and arrows. Archery people understand this. There is a target. There is a bull's eye. When you shoot… you shoot for the bulls eye. If you miss the bull's eye… you miss the mark. The referee would yell… "you sinned". To sin means missing the mark.

This puts a whole different spin on the word *sin*. Have all of us missed the mark at some time? Of course. If we are to be perfect… as God, our Creator, is perfect… then the majority of our lives is spent sinning. We are missing the mark. We are not being the per- son we were created to be. So… we have sinned. Can I forgive myself for missing the mark? YES. Can I forgive others for missing the mark? YES. So… as you let it go… as you release it… as you renounce it… you flush it. It's gone. Do you remember it? NO. It's gone. If you remember it and keep thinking about it… you haven't flushed it.

We are always punished by our sins... not for them. If someone has really done some- thing to you that is gross and awful, they are going to have that come back to them. They will be punished for that. You don't have to worry about it. It's called karma. What goes around… comes around. The Universe remembers the law of balance and order. What we do to others will be done to us. It's not up to us. But… if you take it upon your- self, you are opening the Universe door so that it can come back on you. You don't want to deal with that.

We have the power to release… the power to forgive. That is a great power. Not only do we release them… we release ourselves. This is really the only way to freedom. When we do this, then we put ourselves in harmony. We give love for error. Love is harmony. Love is the balance. We are putting ourselves in harmony and balance.

You and I need to have a clean slate. We cannot have clean slates if we are carrying around the past hurts… all that past stuff. It impedes our journey toward enlightenment.

And… that is really the only journey there is. We have to release all that stuff. There is a power in me called renunciation. I have the power to forgive. I have the power to release.

We have learned that we give truth for error. If someone does something bad to me…what do I do? Do I do something bad back to them? NO. We give them truth instead. What is truth? Truth is love. As you and I get an understanding that we are in a position to free our souls from those past sins… we are freeing our body from disease… which is the effect of sin… missing the mark… error thinking. In the spiritual understanding of I AM… forgiveness means to give truth for error. The mind is now set in order… and the body is healed. The body is merely a mirror of what is going on in the mind. As you let it go… as you forgive… you remember what Jesus said to everyone… *be ye healed... go and sin no more.* The more hurts and resentments that we carry around with us… the more likely we are to have ill health.

This law of renunciation… this law of elimination is a very powerful tool. Every morning we should be doing our forgiveness work. Every evening and every morning we should be recalling things that we are holding on to, and we should consciously release and let it go. If you don't think you can do that then ask the Holy Spirit to help you. Be willing to do it. Do something to release and let go. You cannot believe the freedom that you feel when you are not holding on to the past. We cannot move forward if we carry that baggage of the past.

Our work is to forgive. Every morning… every evening… let it go. You cannot believe how good you are going to feel. It's like when you are carrying luggage around on a trip and you get someplace where you can put it down. What a relief. When we take too much luggage, we swear we will not be bogged down the next time with excess baggage. It is ruining our trip.

When we carry around too much baggage from the past…
it can ruin this trip of life. I release and I let go.

STRENGTH

God is my source and God is my strength.

All things are perfect.

A lot of people confuse power and strength. They are two different attributes. Strength is stickability… the ability to stick with it until it's done. If you have ever watched weight lifters, you will notice that they get themselves all psyched-up. They look around. Then they reach down and they grab the weights. They pull them up to their waist.Then they push them up over their heads. Then they have to stand there with the weighs over their head for a certain length of time. Strength is the ability to hold it up there.

Charles Fillmore said that strength is the freedom from weakness. It is the power to with- stand. It is the capacity to accomplish. Strength originates in spirit. We can spiritually manifest strength. Jesus was the way-shower… the teacher we are striving to follow… not only in a mind culture, but also in a body culture. By faithfully studying what Jesus taught… we find that we can bring forth the very best in ourselves. Through the Christ within us… the mind and the body of all of us have the power of using strength on various planes. We affirm that we are steadfast and strong in thought and in deed.

Imagine that all the cells in your body have little ears. They hear what you say. They can only be and do what they hear you say they are. If you constantly say you are weakand sickly… the ears of you cells hear that. Because we operate under the law of the Universe… we must be what we say we are. That's the way it works. If you constantly say… I am strong… the ears hear that. They respond accordingly. When we understand that… we have it made.

The strength of the Lord is in me.
I am strong.
That's the truth.

Who would imagine that our bodies would do whatever they are told… no matter what the circumstances? That takes strength to do that. We begin to gain in strength when we begin to trust in spirit. The strength of spirit is necessary. The minute we begin to trust spirit… we begin to develop strength. You can relax and let your consciousness do the work for you.

No harm can befall me.

I am made strong through spirit.

The joy of the Lord is the wellspring within me.
I am established in Divine strength.

God is my source.
I am attached to Divine strength.

The minute that you acknowledge that God is your source…
half of the battle is done.
The other half is… let God do it.

Those little ears all over your body are hearing that. They are going to be calling on a strength that is beyond your present comprehension and capacity. Whenever you come on a situation that seems to be challenging for you… acknowledge:

God is my source and God is my strength.

I can feel that moving through my body right now. The more I affirm that… the more that faculty in me develops into a power. Eventually… I will no longer need to affirm that… it is the truth of me. It is my automatic way of thinking and believing. Then… the truth of me is strength. I do not get discouraged. I can stay the course. God is my source and my strength. When we speak of God… we are talking about your father within… your Cosmic Mind. It is developed and it is there for you in every situation.

God is my source and God is my strength.
All things are perfect.

Stickability and being able to stay the course, is a great character trait. I am not talking about staying the course for the sake of being obstinate. Some people will stay on a course just because they said they would… whether it is good for them or not. That is called stubbornness… not strength. There is a difference.

You and I have been given the power to decide what we want to do in life, and that strength to carry it through. But if we haven't developed that power of strength, then we have a difficult time accomplishing anything... doing what we set out to do. Sometimes this is frustrating. Because you say… I want to do this. Why can't I do this? It is because the power of strength has not been developed. It is a spiritual power. You can refuse to let the thought of weakness to enter your consciousness.

You can say a Denial first:

My past weakness no longer has power over me.
I release it and I let it go.
The other way I used to think about myself no longer exists.

You may wonder how Affirmations and Denials can be of help. When Jesus said… *get thee behind me, Satan…* he meant to turn away from wrong-minded thinking. That is a denial. When you affirm that you are hooking into a spiritual power, that you have, you are opening the door for that spiritual power to meet you more than half-way. Like attracts like. It is a power that you have, but… it must be cultivated. Every time you see a weakness, which we will call a weed around the power that you are trying to cultivate, you pluck it out with a Denial. Then, you ask the Holy Spirit to open that door to help me to cultivate the strength in me. It is a power that I am moving from a faculty to a power. I am moving it from a seed to a full-blown plant. I am strong and powerful. Just saying that, begins to activate that power in you… that strength.

Look in the mirror and say the Affirmation:

I am strong.
I am steadfast.
I am cultivating this strength now.

The power of saying that begins to be like fresh, living water on a plant that has been hungry and thirsting to be watered.

We have to acknowledge the truth of ourselves in order to nourish it into existence. We have to know that these powers are in us. You can say:

I am established in Divine strength.

God is my God is my source and God is my strength.

All things are perfect.

UNDERSTANDING

Divine understanding in me unites with the Holy Spirit and I always know what to do.

We are talking about spiritual understanding which is different from intellectual under- standing. It is the ability of the mind to comprehend and realize the laws of thought in relation of one to another. When you have Divine understanding, you really understand the universal laws and you are able to completely comprehend them. It is that something in which we understand the relationship to God and ourselves. If we can understand that… we've got it made.

Understanding reveals that love and wisdom should work together, and that power should be expressed through love. Zeal should be tempered with wisdom. Understanding reveals those things. Some people get it about wisdom but they don't understand that love and wisdom work together. People get it that wisdom means being smart, but that's not what wisdom is. Wisdom and love work together, and power should be expressed through love. Zeal should be tempered with wisdom.

We have to realize that intellectual understanding comes first. We all know what this is. You can read book and you can intellectually understand it. Then… we get into a deeper understanding When we do that… our whole self ripens into wisdom. There is a difference between intellectual understanding and spiritual understanding.

Here is a Bible story: We have heard of John the Baptist. He was the predecessor of Jesus. He was the fore-runner of Jesus. Metaphysically in the Bible... John stands for intellectual understanding or illumined intellect. Illumined means the light bulb has gone off and you get it intellectually. That always comes first. Jesus represents spiritual understanding. That is that understanding that goes into the heart.

Every once in a while we get an ahaaa experience. You have known something intellectually for a long time… but one day you get it on a different level. Then you say… ahaaa… now I understand. Now I get it. Now I see. That means that you clicked from intellectual understanding into spiritual understanding. We all know that John was beheaded. That goes right along with his statement… I must decrease so that He can increase. He is talking about his ministry, but what he is really saying metaphysically is that we must stop thinking with the intellect and begin thinking with the heart. Thinking with the heart… we always think of the heart as being the feeling nature. It is but…we think with our head and feel with our heart. But… when we begin to think with our heart… then we have gone into spiritual understanding.

We can all pray for spiritual understanding about what is going on in the world today. It seems that we are in a great deal of chaos. If we get spiritual understanding, we realize that we are not in chaos. We are in change. Change appears as chaos. The minute we start getting new ideas, it appears in a different way.

Imagine that you decide to clean out your closet. Whenever we clean out, somewhere in the middle… before it is done… it looks worse than it did before we began. Everything is in the middle of the room. Everything appears to be chaotic. But it is not. It is just what has to happen before the change can take place.

Once we clean out… once we get rid of the pile in the middle of the floor… and we put things back… they go back in an orderly way and all of a sudden we take a deep breath and we say… it is done. In the middle of change, it appears to be chaos. That is exactly what is happening in the world today. We are in the midst of change.

We are changing from the Piscean Age into the Age of Aquarius. It has to happen. How do you and I stay sane during this change? We stay sane through our spiritual under- standing that all is well. All is well. Look at this and don't see chaos. See Divine change taking place. During this war aftermath… we are going to need spiritual understanding. Let's affirm together:

Divine understanding in me unites with the Holy Spirit and I always know what to do.

Through that power of the Holy Spirit, you and I have the power to decree and declare. It is called affirmative prayer. We have just affirmed and decreed that Divine under- standing in me unites with the Holy Spirit and I always know what to do. We have set that in motion We have sent it into the Universe. The Universe brings it back with our cup running over.

WILL

Thy will… not mine be done.
I now have a Divinely guided will.

Will can either make us or break us. If that will power in us is developed in such a way that it is ego-driven, we are in for a hard time. That means we are placing our will above every one's. We are saying… you can't change my mind. I know better than anyone else. I have a will of iron.

Will is a power only if it is a rightly directed will. We need to come in with that phrase… *thy will... not mine be done.* That may be the scariest statement in all of Christian-dum… particularly for those people who have a very strong will. They are in control. They don't want to turn their will over to anyone else's. I fell into that category at one time, myself.

Let's talk about what the will of God is. We are talking about Divinely directed will. My will can be Divinely directed. That is what … *thy will...not my will* actually means. We have to understand that *thy will*…or Divine direction…is **always** for our highest good. Suppose we think that our will and God's will are going in the same direction because we both want what is best for me. I think I know what's best for me. I want it now. Maybe God's will is saying… you could have something a lot better than that. Would you even consider something better? You say… no, I want that. That's crazy. Divinely directed will is what we should all be striving for. A reading from *A True Lent* by Charles Fillmore says:

When a man wills the will of God to be done, then they form spiritual character. The use of the regenerative will is for the sole purpose of spiritual enfoldment.

We can do all the things that we think are going to get us there… but the minute we surrender our will to this Divine will… then we make giant steps in our spiritual growth.

We talk about the will of the personality versus Divine will… the will of God. What is the will of God? We have to stop thinking of God as a person. The Divine will of universal energy is harmony and balance… everything fitting together perfectly. When we bring in Divine will, or ask for Divine Guidance in our will, then everything in our life begins to fit together perfectly. Everything is in balance and everything is in harmony.

We wonder if harmony and balance are really the ultimate. What about ecstasy and bliss? Well… harmony and balance bring ecstasy and bliss. When we have problems in our lives, it means that things are not working in harmony. The importance of harmony is not to be minimized. Don't you know when you hear some one hit a wrong note? When something is not in tune? When something is out of harmony, it is not pleasant. That is what happens in out lives. It screeches at us. It makes your skin crawl.

When you have everything working in your life in the Divine will of God, nothing is out of pitch or off key. Everything works in harmony. We should not be addicted to this thing called ecstasy. If you stayed in a state of ecstasy all the time, then that would be the norm and then you would have to go up to a higher level of ecstasy.

We have to learn to live in harmony with ourselves and with others. That does produce a natural state of ecstasy that we don't get tired of. That's what we are all looking for. People are self-medicating these days to get out of pain. You have pain because your life is not in harmony. We learn that the way out is:

Thy will… not mine be done.
I now have a Divinely guided will.

WISDOM

I am filled with light, life, and wisdom.

Wisdom is Guidance from the Holy Spirit. We get flashes of understanding all the time. But Divine Wisdom is spiritual discernment. Because this is a power that we have, we can call it into play. Wisdom is within you and it is of Spirit. It cannot come out until we call it into play. You must ask Holy Spirit for the Guidance. That is calling in Divine Wisdom so that you know what to do. Divine Wisdom is always pure. It is always peaceable. Wisdom is always a win… win situation. It has no ego in it. How can I discern Divine Wisdom from ego-guidance? It changes your way of thinking, and it makes you peace- able. It makes you non-judgmental. It brings solutions into your life that bring you peace.

When we call in Divine Wisdom, we find that we look at things differently, because we are not looking at it from the ego. We are looking at it from Spirit. One of the first things that Divine Wisdom does in us, it helps us to detach. Detachment is a great practice. When we can detach and look at it without our emotion being involved, we get a clearer picture.

How many times have we gotten so riled up and we make the wrong decisions because we are going to do something in spite of someone else… or to spite someone else… just because? We cannot do what needs to be done because our emotions have gotten in the way and cluttered the picture. When we call in Holy Spirit for Divine Wisdom, those emotions somehow go away and we become peaceful so that the decisions we make are righteous.

Righteous does not mean holy… or holier than thou. It means right… in alignment with Spirit. If you are in alignment with Spirit, you can't be wrong. You cannot get in alignment… righteous… if your emotions are pulling you the other way. When you call in Holy Spirit in every situation… before you get all out of whack… just sit with it. Let it just be with you... in you. Say… "I am not going to be upset about this. I am not going to think about this. I am not going to worry about this. I am going to call in Holy Spirit and ask for Divine Wisdom and let it bring me right-minded thinking."

The hardest part for any of us is not the calling in Divine Wisdom. It is taking the time to sit with it. We want to do it, and we want to do it now. We want to do it the way we want to do it. We don't want to give Wisdom time. After you get used to calling Divine Wisdom, and after it begins to work with you at all times, it will pre-empt your confused thinking. You will have opened the door so that every situation in your life will be bathed in Divine Wisdom before you even ask. The Bible says that God knows what we want before we ask.

What we are doing now in learning about these 12 powers, is we are learning that we have the capacity within us. We are learning to call them into action. I am not talking about just calling them in on big things. I am talking about calling them in on everything. How about calling in the parking goddess? Call for guidance in everything you do. How- ever, as you call it in, it begins to make a path to you. Ultimately, you begin to think with Divine Wisdom'

This is a quote from *The True Lent,* by Charles Fillmore:
"As I dwell upon this all-knowing faculty within, I become conscious of the Christ radiance lighting my mind and my whole being is illuminated. My thoughts are quickened through their conscious relationship to spirit."

You are wise beyond your wildest expectations. If you say... no I am not... you are coming from your ego. Ego is not wise beyond your wildest expectations, but Spirit is. Go to your source. Go to spirit for knowledge and understanding... for your wisdom. You are wise. It is a power within you. Call it in today in everything that you do.

As we contemplate this all-knowing faculty, we realize that it is a power to be wise in all situations. It is one of our sources. We can say:

I am filled with light, life, and wisdom.

ZEAL

Today… I sizzle with zeal… the zeal for living.

Feel any different? Zeal means going forward. It means pedal to the metal. It means stomp on the accelerator. **ZOOM**! That's what zeal is. However… it's more than just going forward. It means going forward with great enthusiasm. Zeal is the mighty force that incites all things into action. It is the eternal urge behind all things.

Sometimes we just can't get started. We seem to be stuck. That's because we don't have any zeal. You can pray for zeal to be ignited to get that urge to move forward. It's a zest that we need for living. It's the zest to incite achievement. Zeal is one of those things that is dangerous to us if it's not combined with wisdom. You can get so fired up with zeal that you can burn out. Sometimes you have so much zeal for a particular project that you burn out before you get it finished.

There are a lot of people who are real go-getters in the beginning. You have to be careful when people have too much zeal because at that point it won't last. Zeal gets you started. It's not something that lasts a long time unless it is tempered with wisdom. So… when you are praying for zeal in your life, you also need to pray for wisdom to go along with it.

Zeal has the power to eat things up. When you put something on the stove to heat it up so you can eat it, you want it hot, but you don't want it so hot that you can't eat it. That's the way it is with zeal. You want zeal but you want tempered zeal. We can't just let zeal run wild in us, but we do need it in order to get things started. We've got to have it.

When you build a fire to heat stuff out in the woods, you must have controlled fire. If you have uncontrolled fire, you burn the forest down. You have to be careful with zeal. We need to have zeal to have zest for living. Have you ever gotten into what we might call a ho-hum? That's when we need to pray for zeal. Charles Fillmore had an affirmation that he used even when he was 90. He would jump out of the bed in the morning and say:

I sizzle with zeal… the zeal for living.

He had it. He was going to work at 90. He was writing books. He was thinking. He was operating because he had his zeal. Zeal is something we can all use… particularly in these times. It's easy for us to get discouraged. It's easy for us not to know what to do. That can go into a haze that falls over living, and before you know it… we've lost our zest for life. We say… what's the use? The economy is down. What's the point? When the going gets tough… the tough get going.

The going is tough only if we see it as that. When we call on these 12 powers, we are using the powers that God has given us to withstand all things. These are the powers that we have so that we can live life successfully. I need zeal tempered with wisdom so that I don't go crazy. People with a crazy look in their eye is zeal without wisdom.

How do we know the difference? That is where our faith comes in. We activate zeal by affirming it into power:

My zeal is afire.

I am afire with zeal. Begin to talk about your zeal. Encourage it to come forward.

My zeal is tempered with wisdom and I maintain a perfect balance within and without.

We keep coming back to that word, balance. When everything works smoothly, you have harmony and balance. We want zeal in our life, but we don't want zeal without wisdom. Zeal tempered with wisdom produces harmony and balance in our lives.

We need to realize that we were created to work a well-oiled machine. A well-oiled machine works in balance, and it gets the job done. We are balance. We live in harmony. Isn't that what we want now in the world? Don't we wish that everyone could live together in peace and harmony? You can't have peace and harmony when one part is going wild on you. You have to have balance.

When we pray for peace, we need to be careful what we are praying for. Peace does not mean... stop fighting. We can never stop fighting until there is harmony in the world... so that everyone is equal. Everything has to operate on an equal basis. Can we have zeal for harmony? Yes. You can have zeal for harmony, but... zeal for harmony doesn't mean you are out of control for wanting peace. That's not peaceful.

Do we know what a peaceful demonstration is? How can there be peace unless

it begins with me? I want everyone else to be peaceful, but I'm not going to be. That won't work. There is no peace. Peace means that everybody is at peace. So... when we get too much zeal over wanting peace... there is no peace. Our zeal has run away. It needs to be tempered with wisdom. Our prayer is:

I sizzle with zeal, but my zeal is tempered with wisdom.

Can we sizzle with wisdom? Sure…why not?

I sizzle wit zeal and wisdom.

and I maintain a perfect balance within and without.

CHAPTER FOUR
TRUTHS

EMPOWERMENT

The purpose of this chapter is to tell you that you are a powerful person. You not only can predict & forecast your future, you can create it. Whatever it is that you want to happen, you can cause it to happen. The reason that you are able to this is because of the Laws of the Universe.

Now… there are physical laws of the universe, & there are meta-physical laws of the universe. One of the physical laws of the universe is the law of gravity. The law of gravity says… if you jump off the Golden gate bridge, you are going to get wet. It works every time. One of the meta-physical laws of the Universe is… Thoughts Become Things. It works every time.

On the physical plane, the earth is the matrix into which we plant seeds causing vegetation to grow. And… what you plant is what you get. I remember that my grandmother had a garden in the back yard. She would save the little seed packets & stake each one at the head of each row. At a glance, she could tell exactly what to expect from each row that she had planted. What you plant is what you get. It works everytime.

The earth is an abundant matrix. If you plant one kernel of corn, you get a stalk. The stalk may have 5 ears. Each ear may have 100 kernels. So… by planting 1 kernel, you now have 500 kernels. The earth is an abundant matrix. So… to summarize… on the physical plane, what you plant is what you get, and… you get it in abundance.

On the meta-physical plane, divine substance is the matrix into which we plant our thoughts causing our reality to manifest. And… what you plant is what you get. The way this works is… each thought that you send out is vibrating at a certain frequency. And since like attracts like, the thought finds the reality that is vibrating at the same frequency, grabs onto it, and drags it back in, causing the thought to manifest into that reality. That is the Law of Like Vibration. What you plant is what you get. It works every time,

How many people do you know who frequently say… "I am always tired. I never have enough energy. I wake up tired. I go to bed tired." The universe hears this negative affirmation & sends that person… "always being tired." And… that person gets "always being tired" in abundance. Divine substance is an abundant matrix.

How many people do you know who frequently say… "I am always short of money. I never have enough money to even pay my bills. I am always broke." The universe hears this negative affirmation & sends that person… "always being broke." And… that per- son gets "always being broke" in abundance. Divine substance is an abundant matrix.

On the other hand, you and I know how to use the Law of Like Vibration to our advantage. We know this mantra to be the truth:

AN END RESULT
VISUALIZED WITH EXPECTATION
WILL ALWAYS CREATE THE CIRCUMSTANCES
NECESSARY TO CAUSE ITS MANIFESTATION,
NO MATTER HOW UNLIKELY OR EVEN IMPOSSIBLE
THOSE CIRCUMSTANCES MAY HAVE PREVIOUSLY SEEMED.

This truth of this mantra is vividly illustrated by the story of:

THE DONKEY IN THE WELL

ONCE UPON A TIME, THERE WAS AN OLD DONKEY.
HE LIVED ON A FARM.
HE WAS RETIRED.
HE SPENT HIS TIME FROLICKING AROUND THE FARM.

ONE EVENING, HE FROLICKED TOO CLOSE
TO AN OLD ABANDONED WELL.
HE LOST HIS FOOTING.
HE SLIPPED, & FELL IN... FEET FIRST.

WELL... THERE HE WAS LOOKING UP & THINKING:
"THIS IS NOT WHERE I WANT TO BE."
BEING A METAPHYSICAL DONKEY,
HE KNEW THAT IF HE WAS NOT WHERE HE WANTED TO BE,
HE NEEDED TO VISUALIZE HIMSELF BEING
WHERE HE ACTUALLY WANTED TO BE.

SO... HE VISUALIZED THAT,
IN THE MORNING,
THE FARMER & THE FARM HANDS
WOULD NOTICE HE WAS MISSING,
COME LOOKING FOR HIM, FIND HIM,
& RESCUE HIM.

SURE ENOUGH... THE NEXT MORNING, THE DONKEY HEARD VOICES.
IT WAS THE FARMER & THE FARM HANDS LOOKING FOR HIM.
THE FARMER SPOTTED THE DONKEY IN THE WELL & EXCLAIMED:
"HERE HE IS... IN THE WELL.
I HAVE BEEN MEANING TO FILL THIS HOLE IN FOR A LONG TIME.
THAT OLD DONKEY HAS OUTLIVED HIS USEFULNESS.
WE MIGHT A WELL FILL THE HOLE IN RIGHT NOW."

THE DONKEY WAS PETRIFIED.
THAT IS NOT WHAT HE HAD VISUALIZED.
HE VISUALIZED THE FARMER & THE FARM HANDS RESCUING HIM.

AT THE FARMER'S COMMAND,
THE FARM HANDS GRABBED THEIR SHOVELS
& BEGAN SHOVELING DIRT INTO THE HOLE.

THE DONKEY THOUGHT:
"I AM GONNA BE HARD-PRESSED TO CALL THIS 'GOOD'.
BUT... I'M CALLIN' IT 'GOOD'."

AS THE DIRT WAS SHOVELED INTO THE HOLE,
IT FELL ON THE DONKEY'S BACK.
HE SHOOK IT OFF.
IT FELL ONTO THE FLOOR,
& THE DONKEY TRAMPED ON IT.

AS THIS PROCESS CONTINUED,
THE DONKEY REALIZED THAT THE FLOOR OF THE WELL
WAS RISING TOWARD THE TOP OF THE WELL,
AND... SO WAS HE.
UP, UP, UP, HE WAS GOING.

THE DONKEY THOUGHT:
"HEY... THIS IS GOOD.
THIS IS WHAT I VISUALIZED.
THESE GUYS ARE RESCUING ME."

AS THE PROCESS CONTINUED,
THE DONKEY WAS ABLE TO HOLD HIS HEAD UP HIGH,
LOOK OUT ONTO THE FARM,
STEP UP,
STEP OUT,
AND WALK AWAY.

THE DONKEY WAS ABLE TO WALK AWAY
FROM A CHALLENGING SITUATION.

If you and I are faced with a challenging situation, we call it 'good'. We don't call it 'good' because it is good. NO... NO...NO! We call it 'good' so that it can become good.

As I recite the mantra again, which describes the manifestation process, think of the donkey in the well.

AN END RESULT VISUALIZED WITH EXPECTATION,
WILL ALWAYS FORCE THE CIRCUMSTANCES NECESSARY TO CAUSE ITS MANIFESTATION,
NO MATTER HOW UNLIKELY,
OR EVEN IMPOSSIBLE THOSE CIRCUMSTANCES MAY HAVE PREVIOUSLY SEEMED.

You might be saying to yourself, that story of the **DONKEY IN THE WELL** might be an interesting, fictional story to illustrate the meta-physical law of… Thoughts Become Things. However, it may be far-fetched to imply that it can apply it to OUR real-life day- to-day experiences. To the contrary, it is not far-fetched at all. It works every time.

Four years ago, I was on a 7-day cruise around the Hawaiian Islands. I was part of a 40 member group of devotees of Mike Dooley. Mike Dooley writes a daily e-mail column, entitled, *Notes from the Universe.* He writes as if he were the Universe, addressing the reader. Those of us who were in his group did everything that everyone else did on the cruise. However, in addition, we attended his 3 workshops on how to manifest our thoughts into reality. This is a synopsis of the manifestation process:

MANIFESTATION PROCESS

LIKE ATTRACTS LIKE.
LIKE BEGETS LIKE.
THOUGHTS BECOME THINGS.

WHATEVER YOU WANT,
HOPING, WISHING, BEGGING WILL NOT GET IT FOR YOU.
HERE'S HOW TO GET IT!

AN END RESULT
VISUALIZED WITH EXPECTATION
WILL ALWAYS CREATE THE CIRCUMSTANCES NECESSARY TO CAUSE ITS MANIFESTATION,
NO MATTER HOW UNLIKELY OR EVEN IMPOSSIBLE THOSE CIRCUMSTANCES MAY HAVE PREVIOUSLY SEEMED.

SO... HOW DO YOU VISUALIZE AN END RESULT

WITH EXPECTATION & CAUSE ITS MANIFESTATION?

HERE ARE THE 4 EXCITING STEPS THAT ACTIVATE YOUR MANIFESTING POWER:

1. IDENTIFY... THE END RESULT.

WHILE WANDERING THE YELLOW BRICK ROAD MAY BE EXCITING, DON'T FORGET THAT THE END RESULT IS TO REACH THE LAND OF OZ.

2. FOCUS... ON THE END RESULT.

EXPRESS GRATITUDE THAT THE END RESULT HAS ALREADY HAPPENED. THIS IS FUTURE SPEAKING TO YOURSELF.
THE UNIVERSE REWARDS GRATITUDE WITH ABUNDANCE. DO IT FOR 5 MINUTES EVERY DAY.
SEE EVERY DETAIL. FEEL THE EMOTION.
IT'S YOUR STORY.
PUT YOURSELF IN THE PICTURE. YOU ARE THE STAR.
DON'T MESS WITH THE CURSED "HOWS".
THAT'S NOT YOUR JOB. THAT'S THE JOB OF THE UNIVERSE.
BEHAVE AS IF THE END RESULT HAS ALREADY HAPPENED.
FAKE IT 'TILL YOU MAKE IT.

3. ACT... ON YOUR GUIDANCE.

THE MERRY-GO-ROUND MAY ONLY GO AROUND ONE TIME. GRAB THE BRASS RING WHEN YOU GET THE CHANCE.

4. CELEBRATE... YOUR SUCCESS.

CONGRATULATIONS IN ADVANCE!

When I returned home, I decided to give the **MANIFESTATION PROCESS** a try. I went to my visualization throne, which is a chair in my living room, & I practiced the process every day for 5 minutes as directed. The first step was to come up with an end result that I wanted to manifest. I decided that it would be fabulous, if the $450,000 mortgage on my Rhode Island Street building went away.... vanished. If that were the case, I would no longer have to pay the monthly $2,500 mortgage payment. It would be as if the Universe gave me a monthly $2,500 raise.

I visualized my holding a huge banner reading:

MORTGAGE PAYMENT,
WELLS FARGO $450,000

Then, I visualized the banner going up in smoke… disappearing… gone. During this process, I never once doubted that it would happen. I never once wondered **HOW** it would happen. I did this for approximately 2 months, daily, 5 minutes each day.

One morning, the phone rang & a woman asked if I were James Johnson. I told her yes, that I was James Johnson. She said: "Mr. Johnson, we would like to pay off your $450,000 mortgage to Wells Fargo Bank, & give you $100,000." I said: 'Well, it's about time." After all, I had been visualizing faithfully for 2 months.

I inquired as to the sequence of events that would cause this event to happen. The woman said that she represented a Reverse Mortgage Company. I told her that I was not familiar with how reverse mortgages worked.

She indicated that she knew that I was 72 years old, single, the sole owner of my property & she assumed the property to be worth $1.5 million. Based on my age, & the value of the building, they would loan 40% of the appraised value. She said that I would never have to make another mortgage payment. The mortgage to Wells Fargo Bank would vanish, disappear…. just as I had visualized.

She said that one year after I leave the planet, the building will be sold, & the Reverse Mortgage Co. will collect their $$$ at that time. But, I will not be the one to pay it. After they are paid off, the balance of the sale will go to my heirs.

The woman indicated that to cause the event to happen, their appraiser would need to come & actually appraise the building. The $1.5 million was just a guess. She asked when it would be convenient for their appraiser to come to my house. I said: "Well… we could not possibly do it until this afternoon."

The appraiser came the next day. The building did not actually appraise at $1.5 million. However, it appraised high enough for Wells Fargo Bank to be paid off, & they gave me some spending money, besides.

The purpose of this chapter is to tell you that you are a powerful person. You not only can predict & forecast your future, you can create it. Whatever it is that you want to happen, you can cause it to happen. The reason that you are able to do this is because of the laws of the universe.

Now… there are physical laws of the universe, & there are meta-physical laws of the universe. One of the meta-physical laws of the universe is… Thoughts Become Things.

**AN END RESULT VISUALIZED WITH EXPECTATION
WILL ALWAYS CREATE THE CIRCUMSTANCES NECESSARY
TO CAUSE ITS MANIFESTATION,
NO MATTER HOW UNLIKELY OR EVEN IMPOSSIBLE
THOSE CIRCUMSTANCES MAY HAVE PREVIOUSLY SEEMED.**

IT WORKS EVERY TIME.

PEACE OF MIND

Denial: Nothing around me upsets my peace of mind.
Affirmation: I am always at peace.

People have an idea that peace of mind comes when everything is serene. Wrong. Life is never serene. We can only be serene in life. I often talk about getting your ducks in a row. People always wait until their ducks are in a row before they want to do something. They want to make sure that they have all the facts right before they make a decision. If you are waiting on that… you can forget it because it is not going to happen. There is always life. There is always death. There is always birth. There is always up. There is always down. There is always this. There is always that. That's what it is. The whole key is to become serene and peaceful no matter what happens. That is the key to peace of mind.

Jesus said… *I am in the world, but not of the world.* This is what He is talking about. You and I have to live in this world because we have our earth suits on. We are equipped to be here. We have to become serene and poised and at peace while we are here. We let the earth do what the earth does… which is move around. Everything just moves around. Relationships begin. Relationships end. Babies are born. People die. Stock market is up. Stock Market is down. I get a job. I lose a job. That is the way it is. That is the way it always is.

My job is to be serene while all this is happening. How can I do that? I can only do that when I stand on the rock of God... because it doesn't move. When I know that God is my source… and when I totally understand that there are a set of universal laws that never change… and when I establish my whole self in this… I can be serene. This stuff that is happening out here… it doesn't phase me.

I can take this one step further. Like attracts like. If you are of a chaotic mind-set… what is it that will be going on around you? CHAOS. We have to become peace while there is chaos around us. and then what will happen eventually? It is not really going to change… but our perception of it is going to change. We will not be aware of the chaos that is going on.

I am willing to bet that this has happened to you. Looking at your friends, and your co- workers, who are upset all the time. And you say… what is going on here… I don't really see anything that's that bad… but they do. That peace of mind that you are beginning to establish puts you in a place where you don't even see whatever it is they are so upset about… their chaos. The more serene… the more peaceful that you and I become, then that is what life appears to be for us.

To get started… we have to say as Jesus said…*what is this to me?* Do I care if the Stock Market goes up and down? What do I care? God is my source. God always gives me exactly what I need. Peace of mind allows us to have fun with life. How many people do you know that just don't ever seem to have any fun? What a bummer way to live. Life is supposed to be filled with joy. How can we be joy-filled if we are in a constant state of chaos? We can't.

So… we need to become peaceful. In my church we end every Sunday Service with the Peace Song… let there be peace on earth and let it begin with me. The point is… it has to begin here. It can only begin here when we establish ourselves in God, because God is steady. The confusion around us becomes less when we don't get confused.

Let me tell you… I know that I am always right. That is very comforting. That is because I always ask the Holy Spirit what I need to do. When I say… I am right… I mean that I am right for me. See the difference? Peace of mind comes from asking and receiving, and knowing the truth. I don't have to worry. I don't have to guess. I don't say… I don't know what to do. Stay in the Christ Consciousness… the God Mind… the Holy Spirit guidance. How do we do that? We ask. Ask and you will receive. Ask what you need to know. Ask what decision you need to make. Don't say… show me how to live my life. That will be a little awesome when that comes in. The next thing that happens and you need to make a decision… you say… what do I need to do here? Ask God. Ask the Holy Spirit and you will receive the answer. And then…you do it. Then the next thing happens. You ask. You get the answer, and… you do it. That's how you live life. You don't ask for the big swoop, because we can't take that in. We live a day at a time. We live a moment at a time. We live a decision at a time. The way we have peace of mind is to call in God every time.

We know about the power of the I AM. What is God's name? I AM that I AM. That is what the burning bush said to Moses. I AM so that I can become that. So… whatever I put my I AM to… I am forming and creating that as my reality.

Imagine yourself and what you are putting your I AM to right now. Whatever you put your I AM to… that's what you really believe about yourself. So… if I say… I am always at peace… does that mean at this moment that I am? No. It means that I am creating that. We must decree and declare before it can be.

Now get this: The earth was made for us… not us for the earth. We have dominion over the earth. We have dominion. Therefore… we have to declare and decree how it is to be. We are living it backwards. We let the earth be in charge and then we keep ducking so we don't get hit. We must stand firm and declare and decree. We must say… this is the way it is This is who I am. This is how I live my life… and let the earth then … do it.

That's the way it was meant to be. That seems backwards because we have never been taught that way… the correct way. That's what the God I us is about. I AM that I AM. That is how we create. So… you have to start declaring and decreeing who it is you want to be and what you want and how you see yourself. I AM this way. I AM this way. Then… allow it to be.

So… we declare and decree the peace of mind that is in us because we have established ourselves in God. Establishing yourself in God… think about that. God is… and I AM. If I establish my I AM in what is… that works out to be reality. I AM this. I do this through the power of establishing myself in God. So… that takes the Ego out of it. This way we are not saying I am doing it. No… it is the Father Within that is doing the work. It is the I AM within us that is doing it.

Denial: Nothing around me upsets my peace of mind.
Affirmation: I am always at peace.

I want to read to you from the Book of John. The other Gospels, Matthew, Mark, and Luke are called the synoptic Gospels. They are merely an accounting of events. John is called the Spiritual Gospel. It takes the teachings of Jesus and interprets them in a mystical manner. Unity is a metaphysical church and it teaches a metaphysical interpretation of the scripture… not just the literal interpretation. For that reason, Unity ministers quote from the Book of John more than the other 3 gospels.

Verily, verily , I say unto you…he that believeth on me… works that I do… shall he also do. And greater works than these shall ye do. We will do greater works than Jesus did? Wow! That is what that is saying. Have we been taught to strive to be like Jesus? That sounds almost sacrilegious in some religions. But there it is… right there in the Book of John. We can do miracles?

What Jesus is saying is… if you believe on me as being the spiritual entity that I am teaching you about… if you believe that is in you, too… then greater works will you do. He says the Father and I are one. The kingdom of Heaven is within. I do not do the work. The Father within me does the work. That is what you have to believe. Once you get that… then you can do not only what He did, but greater things.

Let me read you another verse. *The Comforter, whom the Father will send in My name, shall teach you all things and bring all things to your remembrance whatsoever I have said unto you.* That means I don't really need this Bible. It means that I can read this and I can memorize the literal words, but what good will that do? But if you invite the Holy Spirit… the Comforter in… It will teach you all things, and bring all things to your remembrance. Every time you get an aha… it's not like it is something new… it's like you remembered it. You think… I knew that. It's not like it is foreign to you. It's like an awakening to something that's already there.

That's where this remembrance thing comes from. Inside of us… we already know it. But… we have forgotten it. We have become unconscious to the truth, but we have always known it. Why? The Super-conscious Mind…the God Mind…the Christ consciousness… the Father Within… knows it. It's about remembering what you already know. . *The Comforter, whom the Father will send in My name, shall teach you all things and bring all things to your remembrance whatsoever I have said unto you.*

Now… let me quote you the next verse. *Peace, I leave with you. My peace I give unto you... not as the world giveth... give I unto you. Let not your heart be troubled. Neither let it be afraid.* So…He says… I'm going to leave you Peace… but not as the world gives it. So… we say… peace on earth… goodwill to all. We think… everyone is going to stop fighting… everyone is going to stop disagreeing… no more wars. No. He said … I will leave you peace but not that kind of peace.

So… this peace of mind… the place where we can establish ourselves… on that Christ Consciousness… is where we can have peace. That's where it is…. right there on that rock. Then… *let not your heart be troubled. Neither let it be afraid.*

Do we not have peace of mind because we are afraid? We are afraid of what is going to happen… this or that. Well… you don't have to be afraid anymore. You don't have to be troubled anymore. This is a blanket statement… no exceptions. He said… I'm going to leave you My peace. I give it unto you. Here. Where is it going to come from? It is going to come from the Comforter.

If somebody is not at peace and if somebody is afraid… they want comforting… Right? Think of comfort food. It's wonderful, sweet, fattening, and good. It makes you feel good. Now… the Holy Spirit is called the Comforter. What about the comforter on you bed. Don't you just love to snuggle up in it when you want to feel comforted? You wrap up in your comforter.

The Holy Spirit is our Comforter. As we establish ourselves in that, then we can begin to have that peace of mind that we've always sought. In the dictionary… peace of mind is the absence of confusion and conflict in thinking. Always… what we are looking for is the absence of something that is troubling. If we can get rid of the stuff that prevents peace of mind… then what's left? Peace of mind. So… we don't have to search after peace of mind. All we have to do is release confusion and conflict that is in our thinking.

So… we say… OK… I have to live in this world. That is difficult because the world is always changing its mind about what it wants and needs. It's this way one day and it's that way the next. What do they want from me? Well... it's always going to be that way. But… as you and I live in this world… it's about overcoming difficulties or achieving goals. We cannot do that as long as we are stymied with confusion.

It does not matter what it is that you need to know. You are confused… what to do... what to do. This is what you do. You ask. You ask the Holy Spirit. You ask the Comforter... who will bring you all information. Back to the Bible… *It will teach you all things.* So… if you have a question for which you need to know the answer… to the Comforter is where you go. Don't look out there. It's going to change its mind. Before you get around to doing it… it will have switched.

sSo… you say… OK… Holy Spirit… what is it that I need to do right now? The Holy Spirit is going to tell you. It may not be a voice out of the clouds. But… there will be something. It may come as an intuition. It may be on the side of a bus as it goes by. You say… how can that be? But… it just happens. What you and I have to do then… is act on it.

We get the information… now what?

Mistake #1: Do nothing.

We try to calm everything down in our lives. We try to assess everything. If you know you may run into a conflict… you just don't do that anymore. You avoid that issue… not realizing that that issue will pop up in the next situation. It will have a funny way of moving around… that thing that you are avoiding. So… you cannot avoid dealing with life. Life is about action… not avoiding. We cannot become so complacent with everything that is going around us that we just stop acting. You say… I won't do anything. I'll just do nothing. Then I won't get the hard knocks. It doesn't happen like that. People that are like that are buried somewhere. When nothing is ever happening in you life… that means that you are dead, because… there is always going to be this stuff going on. We have to begin to live and we have to look at every challenge as an opportunity to overcome. Overcome means to go over it… not through it. Overcoming means going up. Going up means rising to the next level of consciousness. Don't avoid the issue.

Mistake #2: Sit on it.

We find out what we need to do. We've got that. Then… we sit on it. We know what to do. But we don't do it. Why don't we do it? We don't do it because it's going to cause waves. I might lose a friend. Someone may not agree. So… we don't act. The conflict continues. What we have to learn is that we must detach ourselves from other people. We say love one another and all that. You can love one another without being joined at the hip. You've got to let go… and let God. Your children… your

POVERTY IS NOT A VIRTUE

I have mentioned before that you and I have a power within ourselves that enables us to do great things. The Bible tells us that Jesus said...*I have come that they may have life, and that they may have it more abundantly.* That may have been Jesus talking. However, sometimes he chose to talk as a person and sometimes He talked as His Consciousness. That is to say… He spoke as the Christ. He also said...*It is not I who doeth the work...it is the Father within.* He also said…*These things that I do, you will do, also.*

This means that within each one of us there is a Christ that must be developed consciously so that we can live the life that we were intended to live. Let's say that each one of us was born with the intention to live a full and happy life… to glorify that part of our- selves that makes it possible to lead such a life. As you begin to develop the power within you, you begin to understand that all the spiritual and the mental and the material riches of this world are gifts of that power. They are good in themselves and capable of productive use for us.

That power that dwells within us, has been called many names:
Father Within, Christ Consciousness, God Mind, Super-Conscious Mind.
For this presentation… we will call it… the Power Within.

The Power Within will enable us to see clearly that all of these infinite riches are in us as much as all around us. So by learning to use these spiritual laws, then we can extract from these infinite treasures within each of us just what we need in order to live this glorious and abundant celebration of life.

There are times when it seems that this realization is too complicated for us to under- stand. When it gets too complicated for us… we have to realize that we have immediately gone back to coming from the Ego… our little self. The people that boast about being able to do ANYTHING, often times it is their Ego that is talking. But when you realize that you can accomplish anything yourself… using your Power Within… you take a totally different attitude.

You and I were born to do this. And we're no different from anybody else. Every person on the planet was born to do this. So… you can't really take any pride in being able to do it. It is the ability and it is the eternal gift that all of us have. So… when you learn to use this gift properly and begin to grow rich beyond your wildest dreams… you are not taking anything away from anyone else. You are simply developing your own gift.

What we have to really develop is that feeling of unity with this Power in our hearts. That's what makes us rich. If we never even materialized anything from this Power… we would still feel rich. It is our feeling of oneness with God that is the abundance that we are all looking for. This is a mental attitude and a faith that is present in all things. All the riches of this infinite power are great and are available right here for all of us to enjoy.

Let me tell you something right now. **There is no virtue whatsoever in poverty**. It is not a good thing to be poor. This means that you haven't learned to use the ability that is within you in order to achieve what you want. We are here to find our true place in life and to give our talents to the world. We are put on this planet to blossom, to expand, and to unfold in a wonderful way according to this potential that is within us.

You and I need to bring forth all of these spiritual, mental and material riches which will bless humanity and will bless this world. What does the world need now? The world needs for you and me to develop our spirituality. When we do that, we know the Power is in us and we can then create whatever is needed in the moment.

This is our Divine right… to create the infinite the infinite riches within us. This is a Universe of law and order, and there are principles on which these experiences rely. This really is God, our Power Within, as principle…as law. Think about God as a Power, not as a person. Take that skin off of God. This science that I'm talking about is based on the principle of Universal Power. So… as you and I connect with that feeling of oneness with this Power, then… and only then… is when we truly create.

The only law of life is the belief in this Power, and the belief is to sincerely accept that it is the truth. Believe in the abundant life… the happy life… the successful life. Live in the joy and the expectancy of the best. You say it and it is true. You believe it and it hap- pens. That's the power that you have. And the key is this feeling of oneness, of unity, with the God of your life. Once you have achieved that feeling, then it is yours.

Do not say: I can do ANYTHING!

That is not true.

**However you can do anything through you …
through your Power Within**

THE BOOK OF THOMAS

The hidden sayings of Jesus

The Gospel of Thomas was not included in the New Testament in 313AD. The original manuscripts were found in an earthen jar along the banks of the River Nile in 1947 in Nag Hammadi, Egypt. This discovery has given Christianity a whole new slant.

It is what **Unity** and **A Course In Miracles** have been saying all along.

The complete sayings were published in Beyond Belief, The Secret Gospel of Thomas by
Elaine Pagels in 2003.
This book is worth reading.

The selected sayings of Jesus, published here, as found in the Gospel of Thomas are in *italics*.

Whoever unlocks the meaning of these sayings… shall not see death.

If your leaders say to you... look... the Kingdom is in Heaven... then the birds of Heaven will precede you. If they say to you... it is in the sea... then the fish will precede you. Remember... the Kingdom is inside you, and it is outside you.

First of all… we are not talking about the Kingdom of Heaven. It's the Kingdom. Where is the Kingdom? It is inside you, and outside you. The Kingdom is all there is. If the Kingdom is both inside you and outside you… there is no place the Kingdom is not. You are the Kingdom of God. Are you all of the Kingdom of God. NO. But… you are the Kingdom of God.

The Kingdom has to have a King. You cannot have a Kingdom without a King. If this power is inside me... then I have to be the King. If this Power is outside of me… then there is a bigger King. We know that like attracts like. So… what is inside me… must be totally attuned to what is outside me if I am going to attract it. We are talking about the Power.

I don't need to look anywhere for my Power. I do not have to look anywhere for the King of me. It is in me. Suppose when you were growing up… you were told that the Power that runs you is in you. Suppose somebody had told you that. You would be a totally different person today. You are being told that now. So… we need to re-learn.

What is learning? Learning is doing something over and over until it just sprouts forth from you. You can't go back to the book you studied to learn it. You need to have it down pat. You need to know it. Do you know that the Power of the Universe is in you? Do you know that? You say… YES. Well… if you know that… why aren't you using that? If you have the Power of the Universe in you…you have the power to do anything.

When you know yourselves… then you will be known. You will understand that you are children of the Living Father. But... if you do not know yourselves… then you dwell in poverty and you are the poverty.

When you know yourself… that means that you know that you are a spiritual being. If you know that you are a spiritual being… then you will be known. By whom will you be known? You will be known by the Kingdom that dwells outside of you. I must know that I am spiritual in order to be known by the spiritual.

Suppose you are holding a hair dryer. Also suppose that you have no idea what the thing on the end of the cord is. It is an electric plug, but you don't know what it is or what its function is. You are told that the hair dryer will dry your hair. So… you stand there holding the hair dryer up to your hair and nothing happens. Remember... you have no clue about the plug. Now… when you know what the plug will do if it is plugged into the electrical source… and when you plug it in… the hair dryer works.

The minute that we know that we have the Power… that we are the Power… then we will be known. In other words… we can plug into the outside Power and it will run its cur- rent and power through us. It will recognize us and will know us when we know to plug in. Once you know yourself… you will be known. If you don't know what that plug is… you will stand there forever, and never get your hair dry.

When you know yourself… then you will be known. You will understand that you are children of the Living Father. Living means that it is active now, and that you can pull power from it… now. You can pull Spiritual Power from that source. But first… you have to know who you are. You have to know that you can do that.

If you do not know yourself… then you dwell in poverty. You are the poverty. That means that I do not get to use the Power that is available to me and I am poor in spirit. Know what is in front of your face and what is hidden from you will be disclosed to you. For there is hidden that shall not be revealed.

Understanding what this means is a key to your success. First of all… you need to under- stand the meaning of the word… denial. Denial is not a river in Egypt. Denial means that you do not see something. Denial does not mean that you see something and refuse to accept it. NO. Denial means that you do not see it. Denial is a blind spot for you. Every- body else can see it. But… you don't see it. It is in front of your face. But… you don't see it. *Know what is in front of your face and what is hidden from you will be disclosed to you.* That is what Jesus is saying.

If there is anything in your life that you don't want to deal with… you may have removed it from your Conscious Mind. However… it is in your Sub-Conscious Mind. If it is not in your Conscious Mind… to you it does not exist. So… you don't see it. That is the block that keeps you from seeing the big picture of your life. If you can see that blind spot… that thing that you are in denial about… you will remove the block to your growth and achievement. How do you get to see that? We will get to that.

Let's talk about Prosperity. You want to grow in Prosperity. But… no matter what you do… you can't seem to get ahead. You have read… all things are possible to me. You say… that's not true for me. I'm not getting it. What is wrong? What's wrong is that blind spot that you cannot see. It is the block that you refuse to see. The minute that you see it and remove it… your prosperity will come to you.

God always says… YES. You always get what is the dominant energy in your mind. The dominant energy always wins. If you want something and you want it more than you think you don't deserve it… you will get it. If you want something and you think you don't deserve it more than the wanting of it… you will never get it. Usually that not deserving… that reason why it shouldn't happen… resides in your blind spot. That's why you don't see it.

The people around you can see what you are doing or what you are not doing that is blocking you. It is in front of your face. But… you don't see it. That is what Jesus is talking about.

Hanging over the Greek temples of old is the saying: KNOW THYSELF. That is exactly what Jesus is saying. What is my blind spot? What is it that I don't see? Of greater importance… how do I get to see it?

<u>You can ask your best friend.</u> It may or may not be a good idea for him to tell you. First of all… you are not going to believe it. Also… you may lose a best friend.

<u>You can go to therapy</u>. The purpose of going to therapy is to allow a disinterested party to help you see your blind spot. Usually that process takes a lot of sessions and costs a lot of money.

<u>Ask the Holy Spirit for guidance.</u> You will not lose your friends and you will not have to pay for the therapy. Ask God to reveal to you what it is. Use whatever term you want… Holy Spirit, God, Higher Self, Father Within. Whatever term you use is not the problem. The problem is… it will be revealed and you don't believe it. Now you are into the other type of denial… you see it, but refuse to accept it.

When you ask… you are actually asking yourself. Your Sub-Conscious Mind already knows what it is. If you ask for it to be reveled to you… *there is nothing hidden that shall not be revealed.* That is what Jesus was talking about.

When you have a particular problem… you say… what is it that I need to see here? Ask your Higher Self… what am I not seeing here? Many people don't want to do this, because they know they are not seeing it so they can perpetuate the problem. Why do people want to perpetuate the problem? They don't want to see what they don't want to see. That is why it is a blind spot in the first place.

Solomon was reputed to be the world's richest King. He had wealth beyond comparison. How did he acquire untold wealth? Did he pray for untold wealth? NO. He prayed for greater understanding... ultimate understanding… Divine understanding. That is a prayer saying… reveal to me what I need to know. What comes with that? Untold wealth. Wealth of thinking…wealth of perfect health…wealth of prosperity…wealth of relationships. Wealth comes to you when you know what it is that you need to see. When you can say… Ahaaa… now I see it. Then… you have seen. Your Higher Self will reveal it to you when you sincerely ask to have it revealed. Don't let the not wanting over-power the wanting. God always says: **YES.**

The Pharisees and the scribes have taken the keys of knowledge and have hidden them. They have not entered nor have they allowed those who want to enter to do so. As for you… be as shrewd as snakes and as innocent as doves.

Who are the Pharisees and the scribes? They are the keepers of the knowledge. Today… we have keepers of the knowledge. We just have different labels for them. The scribes were the ones who wrote it down and the Pharisees were the ones who said it. The Pharisees were supposed to know all the laws. So… people began to rely on the Pharisees and the scribes. They figured… they are the learned ones. They must know the truth. People paid attention to them.

But… Jesus said… *The Pharisees and the scribes have taken the keys of knowledge and have hidden them. They have not entered nor have they allowed those who want to enter to do so.* Does that apply to today? YES…INDEED! It says… the people we look up to as the learned ones have put us in opposition. They know… just listen to them. Once again, Jesus says… *they have taken the keys and have hidden them.* They haven't gone in and they are preventing others from going in. The lesson for today is… I'm not sure that those people who are telling us what is good for us… know what's good for us.

The Pharisees and the scribes of today have not studied what is going to work for us today in the new millennium. And… if they do have pertinent information… they are withholding it and are distorting it for their own selfish gain. Things that worked in 1950 don't work today. The Pharisees and the scribes of today are going by what worked in 1950. They don't know what will work today and they don't want us to know either.

The Pharisees and the scribes of today must be people who put knowledge, learning, new thought and new ways of doing things… FIRST… so that we can look up to them. If they refuse to enter the house of knowledge… and they won't let anyone else enter the house of knowledge… that is a problem. Do we have that problem today? What do you think? That was a problem in Jesus' day, and that is a problem today.

Given that… what are our instructions? We should be as shrewd as snakes and as innocent as doves. The snake has suffered a bad rap in Christianity. It comes across as the tempter. However… what did that snake tempt Eve to do… to bite of the fruit of the tree of knowledge. Before Christianity… the snake represented wisdom. And… wisdom was always the healer. The symbol for a doctor is a snake wrapped around a staff. Wisdom… knowledge is always the healer. This has nothing to do with politics. Mrs. Kerry responded to a question in which they were trying to trap her into something and she said… "You know… it's always better to know than not know." That's wise. When you know something… you can do something about it. If you don't know… you have no power, at all.

So… the snake represents knowledge. That means that we must be seekers of knowledge. That can be metaphysical knowledge… self knowledge… or knowledge in general. Along with that… we must be innocent as doves. We are not arrogant. We are seekers of knowledge, and wisdom.

Knowledge and wisdom does not necessarily mean book-smart. It's OK to be book-smart. But… that's just half of it. When you are a seeker of wisdom and knowledge… you are seeking within yourself for the truth. If the scribes and the Pharisees have taken the keys of knowledge and have hidden them… and they have not entered and they have not allowed those who want to enter to do so… you have to take matters into your own hands. Don't take anyone's word for something. Do you own investigating. This is a time in history. If you are going to succeed… you have to have the knowledge. We are living in the age of enlightenment. We are living in the age of information. The Age of Aquarius is the age of information. We have moved from the Piscean Age into the Age of Aquarius. It is time that we took those keys of knowledge back.

Knowledge is for everyone. Knowing is for everyone. You cannot solve whatever is going on in your life if you don't know what is going on. Don't depend on what some- body else tells you what is going on. Ask for Divine Guidance. That is the key to knowledge. That is the key to success.

The scribes and the Pharisees have taken the keys of knowledge and have hidden them, and they do not want to go in and they do not want you to go in either. That saying applied in the time of Jesus and it applies to us today.

You and I cannot live… this nation cannot live… this world cannot live using the laws that were enacted in the 1950's. It's a new day. It's a new time. Your life is in your hands. Your future is in your hands. Every problem that needs to be solved must be viewed in a different way than it was viewed in the past.

A person cannot mount 2 horses or bend 2 bows. A servant cannot serve 2 masters or that servant will honor one and offend the other.

There is a right way and a wrong way to do something. I am not saying good and evil. I am saying right and wrong. People who are not living life are constantly trying to stay in the middle... straddle the fence. They are trying to mount the 2 horses. They are trying to do both the right and the wrong. They are trying to serve the 2 masters. It takes intestinal fortitude to know what is right and then to do it. It is one thing to know what to do. It is another thing to do it. A good Affirmation is: I know what to do and I do it.

No person drinks aged wine and immediately desires to drink new wine.

Aged wine has a mature taste that new wine does not have. If you begin to operate from your Higher Self... you are operating from the wisdom within you. Once you begin to operate from that mode of your being... you are not going to want to operate from your ego state of consciousness. That is no longer satisfying to you. A person who drinks aged wine no longer wants the taste of new wine. If you begin shopping at Neiman Marcus... you no longer want to shop at Sears. Once you begin to live life as it was meant to be lived... coming from your inner strength and power... you have no taste for anything less.

New wine is not poured into aged wine skins or it might break. The aged wine is not poured into new wine skins or it might spoil. Old Piscean thinking and ways of doing things will no longer work in the Age of Aquarius. It's a whole new ball game. You can't put a new way of thinking into an old way of doing things. When you begin to see life through the eyes of your inner power... and through the eyes of your prosperity...you cannot put that into your old way of doing things. When you see and think differently... you will do things differently. The new wine will not fit into the old wine skin.

An old patch is not sewn onto a new garment...for...there would be a tear. The old thinking is worn out and it cannot keep up with the vitality of the new. *One who knows all but is lacking in one's self...is utterly lacking.*

What you think of yourself is what you have programmed yourself to be. The True You is in you. It is that spirit part of you. It is the Father Within. It is your Cosmic Mind. It is your Higher Self. That is what you need to tune into.

The saying means that it does not matter if we have a triple Doctorate Degree, or that we know with expertise what we do for a living. All of that is for naught if we are lacking in our- selves. If you are lacking in your contact with your Cosmic Mind... you have nothing.

The Sears Catalogue looked good until you discovered a Neiman Marcus Catalogue. All was well until your limited exposure suddenly became broader. Your desires suddenly became elevated. Your thinking and your expectations reached a higher level. Before you knew about Neiman Marcus… Sears was as good as it got. You were perfectly happy. But… you didn't know what you were missing.

If you have never experienced a spirit-filled life… you are impressed with the wrong catalogue. If all you know is your lower self… you have not really lived yet. When you tune into your Cosmic Mind… you realize that you have been missing out. That is what Jesus meant when he said: *One who knows all but is lacking in one's self is utterly lacking.*

If you bring forth that which is within you... what you have will save you. If you do not have that which is within you... what you do not have within you will kill you.

This puts a whole new spin on the evangelical notion of "being saved". Jesus said: *What is within you...that is what will save you.* He is referring to your Cosmic Mind within you. We need to awaken the Spirit that is within each one of us. That Spirit that is within us will guide us in everything that we do. Whatever your dilemma… your inner guidance of your problems. It will lead you into prosperity, perfect health and peace of mind. It is available for your needs of the moment. It will even see that you find a parking place.

We are talking about celebrating life. What you specifically need to celebrate your life… that is what your Inner Guidance is ready, willing and able to provide. This is not some- thing that you get from a book. It is something that you have to tune in and turn on to.

If you do not have that which is within you... what you do not have within you will kill you. If you are not living life to the fullest… you are considered dead. If you are only living in the lower catalogue… the upper catalogue part of your life is dead. You don't know about it. It does not exist.

Jesus is saying that all we have to do is open ourselves to the Power Within each of us. You don't need to know how to do it. Just say… I am open and receptive to receiving God's truth within me. Open your mind to receiving unlimited possibilities in every aspect of your life. Spirit within you is just waiting to come and be your salvation.

If 2 make peace with each other in a single house... they will say to the mountain...move from here... and it will move.

If 2 make peace with each other in a single house… In the Bible we read a lot about a house divided cannot stand. We also read that you cannot serve God and

Mammon. We also realize that when the Conscious Mind, and the Sub-Conscious Mind disagree… nothing gets done.

We have 3 phases of mind: the Conscious Mind… where our awareness resides… the Sub-Conscious Mind… where our habit patterns are stored… our autopilot… our belief system, and the Cosmic Mind… the Father Within. The Cosmic Mind is perfect and is all-knowing. We only need to be concerned about the other 2 minds being in agreement. In one house means one body… our temple. When 2 in a single house agree… Jesus is talking about the Conscious Mind and the Sub-Conscious Mind being in agreement.

The Sub-Conscious Mind can be programmed in a number of ways. Parents have a lot to do with that with what they tell their children. This can be positive programming or negative programming. The child is open and receptive and they accept what they are told and make that their belief system.

The Conscious Mind… striving for success… may not be in agreement with the negative programming of the Sub-Conscious Mind. The 2 minds probably are not aware that they are not in agreement. Those are the 2 in the one house that must agree.

We need to be aware of what is in our Sub-Conscious Mind so that we can get in agreement with our Conscious Mind, so that we can move that mountain. If we don't like what is in our Sub-Conscious Mind, we can reprogram it so that it is has the answer that will lead you out

We are in agreement with what we want it to be. If these 2 minds are not in agreement as to who we are, we are powerless. If my Sub-Conscious Mind says, you are a great success, and my Conscious Mind says that also, that will move the mountain.

You need to pray… declare…and decree for your Cosmic Mind to reveal to you what you need to know about yourself… what is in your Sub-Conscious Mind. If we want to make a success of our lives… our Conscious Mind and our Sub-Conscious Mind must be in agreement. You cannot fix something if you don't know that it is out of order. You don't know to look there because it is on a sub-conscious level… beneath your Conscious Mind.

If 2 make peace with other in a single house…they will say to the mountain…move form here…and it will move. If you are going to be prosperous… your Sub-Conscious Mind will have to agree with your Conscious Mind that you are prosperous, or you will never be prosperous. Ask your Cosmic Mind to reveal to you what is keeping you from your prosperity. Whatever it is… it is dwelling in your Sub-Conscious Mind and it is in conflict with the desires of your Conscious Mind. When the 2 Minds are in agreement… you can move that mountain… called prosperity. You will move it from this side to that side.

Why did Jesus use the term…mountain? A mountain is symbolic of an obstacle that is hard to overcome. We need to move what is hard to overcome about prosperity. You are the only one who can do it. And… this is how you do it. If 2 make peace with each other in a single house… they will say to the mountain… move from here… and it will move.

THE COLLECTIVE CONSCIOUSNESS

HOW IT WORKS

Each of us has an awareness and each of us has a consciousness. The awareness resides in the Conscious Mind. The consciousness resides in the Sub-Conscious Mind. There are many levels of a Collective Consciousness. Each Collective Consciousnesses represents the average consciousness of its respective domain.

For example… there is a Collective Consciousness of the Universe… of the United States… of California… of San Francisco… of Potrero Hill. The Collective Consciousness for China would look different from the Collective Consciousness of the United States. The residents of Nob Hill would vibrate at a different Collective Consciousness than the residents of the Tenderloin. The employees of IBM would vibrate at a different Collective Consciousnesses than the employees of McDonald's.

HOW WE ARE INFLUENCED BY THE COLLECTIVE CONSCIOUSNESS

We tend to identify to some degree with the Collective Consciousnesses of where we live and work. That is called our Comfort Zone. However… we do not want to adopt the Collective Consciousnesses of our Comfort Zone. Our consciousness is probably vibrating at a higher level than the average, *the mean*, Collective Consciousnesses of where we live and work.

You do not want the Collective Consciousness to run your life. The collective believes in limitation. The collective believes in poverty. If you let the collective run your life… then you are going to manifest in your life exactly what the collective believes. Our consciousness resides in our Sub-Conscious Mind. That is what we want to run our lives. We have control over our Sub-Conscious Mind.

e can easily be influenced by the collective. If we are weaker than the people we are around… we will pick up on their thoughts. If you don't run your Sub-Conscious Mind, yourself… then someone else is going to run it for you.

If you are not going to be yourself… then who is going to do it?

Are you and I run by the Collective Consciousness? In some cities, like New York and San Francisco, many people do not have cars and they are dependent on using the bus for transportation. If you get on the bus… that bus is going to take you where *it* goes.

Chances are… the bus is not going to take you to your front door. You will have to get off at the stop nearest your front door and that may not be near at all. You may have a lot of walking to do. That is not the same as driving your car on the exact route you would like to travel.

The Collective Consciousness that we live in takes us approximately where we want to go. It may also take us through some neighborhoods that we would rather avoid. But when you are on the bus… you go where the bus goes… like it or not. However… you do have a choice. If you don't like the bus you are on… you can always hop off.

Now… I would rather be riding the bus in San Francisco rather than riding the bus in Joplin, MO… where I came from. When I go back to Joplin… I don't even know my way around any more. My consciousness is vibrating at a different level than it used to. I have a different Comfort Zone. Once again… even riding the bus in San Francisco does not take me exactly where I want to go. That is why we need to be awake to ourselves all the time. If we go to sleep… we will allow the collective consciousness to take over.

If you are not going to be yourself… then who is going to do it?

There are people in my Collective Consciousness who believe in lack. There are people in my Collective Consciousness who believe in sickness. I do not want to be taken there. I am working to keep myself on a path of truth so that truth can manifest in my life. Truth is absolute reality. It is that there is only good in this life. There is only God in this life. There is only one Power, and it is God. There is only one Presence, and that Presence is love. I am trying to wake up to that reality.

We need to be our own Captain. We need to guide our own ship. There is no one who will get us there but ourselves. God has already given us everything that we could ever want. We do not need beg for it. NO. We need to wake up to the fact that it is already ours. The Collective Consciousness is not awake to that fact... yet. It thinks that we have to struggle for what we get.

Don't let the Collective Consciousness take over your consciousness.
It will not take you to where you want to be.
Don't get on the bus.

HOW WE INFLUENCE THE COLLECTIVE CONSCIOUSNESS

Are you tired of the bickering that is going on in Washington, DC? Let me remind of something. That bickering that is going on in Washington, DC… is a reflection of the consciousness of you and me. It's us. It's a projection of us. It is a mirror of us. Every- thing that happens out there… particularly in Washington, DC… the

Capital of our country… is a mirror of the Collective Consciousness of our country… not vice-a-versa.

We are always hoping to get a leader who will lead us out of all of this. Well… the leader is you and I. You and I are the ones who will lead us out of all of this. When a leader seemingly comes… he will be a reflection of the leader in us.

Are you mad all the time? Is everything irritating you? Well… that's why things are the way they are. It is a time for us to realize Peace. Once we are peaceful beings in our- selves… once we are at Peace in our hearts… Washington, DC will be at Peace. The world will be at Peace. You may say: Well… that puts a lot on me. Well… where else should it be?

It is a lot better to be responsible than to be the victim. That is the beauty part of what Unity teaches. You and I call the shots. That's the freedom of it all. Unity believes that the entire Universe and everything in it had its beginning in an idea. We believe that everything that we can see and touch is a manifestation of the inter-action between the God Mind and our Cosmic Mind within.

The God Mind is all possibility. It is filtered through the Cosmic Mind of human beings and goes out the other side as reality. Whatever ideas that you and I have are manifested into reality through the God Mind that we access through our Cosmic Mind. In a very real sense… you and I have created our individual experiences, and the Collective Consciousness has created the collective experiences. The experiences merge with the experiences of all other human beings and that creates the world that you and I live in.

WE CREATE OUR OWN REALITY. TOGETHER…
WE CREATE THE REALITY OF THE WORLD.
WE ARE CREATORS… NOT VICTIMS.

WHAT TO DO

Ministers baptize people. What happens in a baptism? The minister gives the person a name. The minister says: *I baptize you (name) in the name of the Father the Son, and the Holy Spirit.* This is a declaration and a decree.

We can baptize events. If something has not happened the way you want it to… baptize that event and give it a name. Once you give it a name… then it becomes that. I baptize this event *success*. If you have something in your life that you want to succeed… baptize it *success*. Baptize it in the name… in the nature of the Father, the Son and the Holy Spirit… which is love… which is success… which is total truth. That is where we want to go. Life is what you name it… what you declare and decree it to be.

Right now…let's baptize this day.
I baptize this day to be success, prosperity, and love in the name of the Father, the Son, and the Holy Spirit.
And so it is.
Amen and Amen

THE MYRTLE FILLMORE STORY

Life is good. I feel fabulous. Just saying that tells my body how to feel. Our body is nothing but little ears... ears that have 20/20 hearing. The cells in our body hear how to be. Our body then responds and becomes that. You may say… *that's ridiculous. The cells don't know.* Well… our body does what it's told to do. In fact… we do what we are told to do.

I am talking Truth.

If you tell a child, over and over, that he is clumsy… and if he buys into it… and if the message gets imbedded into his Subconscious Mind… he will become clumsy… and you are contributing to making his clumsiness a reality. If you tell your body often enough that you feel bad… that you are sickly… that your constitution is not that strong… not as strong as other people's… then… your body becomes that.

Our bodies and beings become what they hear from us and what they hear from others. It is not that easy to un-tell. However… it can be done. If the body is told something that is not the truth… it can be un-told. That is the foundation of *Unity*. It is the story of how *Unity* began.

It is the story of Myrtle Fillmore.

Myrtle Fillmore was the co-founder of Unity, along with her husband, Charles Fillmore. In the late 1800's not much was going on with medicine. At that time…Tuberculosis was a killer…a death sentence. There was nothing anyone could do for Tuberculosis. You were considered dead once you got it. It was the AIDS of its day. Myrtle Fillmore was told that Tuberculosis ran in her family. It probably did run in her family because every- one expected it to. So… she got it.

You and I live with our expectations. People who are told and believe… heart trouble runs in our family… or, the men in our family die at age 50… you are setting up your heart trouble and you are setting up your death at age 50. The ears of the body hear and they comply with what they are told to do.

Myrtle Fillmore was told that she had Tuberculosis. She bought it. So… she got it. She was also told that she had about 6 months to live. She was in her mid-30's. She was married to Charles Fillmore and she had young children. She was preparing for her inevitable death when she went to a lecture by a man named, Dr. Weeks. He was teaching New Thought.

He made a statement that she heard for the first time:

We are children of God.
We are perfect in every way.

She went home and she thought about that. She said… if I am a child of God… and I am perfect in every way… then I cannot have inherited a disease. This disease cannot run in my family because I am a child of God, and God is perfect in every way.

That does not mean that everyone is perfect physically. NO. We are spirit. We are not our bodies. Our spirit is perfect in every way. Our spirit doesn't need saving. There is nothing to save… nothing that needs saving. We are perfect. We are children of God. Because we live in this human body… we are susceptible to hearing things that aren't perfect… and we believe them.

We have a choice.

Myrtle Fillmore had been given misinformation. She bought it, and she got it. Her body believed it. Her Sub-Conscious Mind bought it. The Sub-Conscious Mind believes what- ever it is told. That can be the good news and it can be the not-good news. It brings about whatever it believes. Whatever you believe in your Sub-Conscious Mind about your- self… that is what is manifested into reality. Myrtle Fillmore had been told this enough. She believed it about herself. She created it… a deadly disease... only 6 months to live.

Now…Myrtle Fillmore is saying… *that is not the truth.* She began to re-educate herself. She began to un-learn everything she had thought was true. She began to un-learn that her body has Tuberculosis. She sat down every day in a chair. She put a chair opposite her. She began to picture herself in that chair opposite herself. She began to talk to her- self…just as though she were another person. She said… *you know...I know what you have been taught. But... that is not the truth. Let me tell you what the truth is.*

She began to instruct her body. She praised her body. She said… *you are so good at creating what you believe to be true. I know that you will be able to create what is really the truth. I know you will. You are such a good body. You are so great. The truth is ... you are whole and perfect in every way. You are healthy. There is nothing wrong withyou.*

She sat down every day for 30 minutes and she talked to her body. Her body… with its little ears… began to hear what she was saying. She would not allow anyone around her to speak of her having an illness. They referred to her as whole and perfect in every way. As she began to re-educate her body… her body began to change. It took her approximately 7 years to heal herself. She didn't just say... *you're whole and perfect* and let it go at that. NO.

It takes time and effort to turn things around.

The rest of the story is... Myrtle Fillmore was in her mid-30's... she was given 6 months to live... and she lived to be in her mid-80's. She overcame a terminal illness that medicine had no way to cure. That is a living testimony.

You can re-educate yourself on anything that you want to change. Anything that you want to change about yourself... you need to instruct your body and instruct your mind that they have been given misinformation. Get the correct information... the truth... that you want to feed into your body and into your Sub-Conscious Mind. Take the time to do it every day.

It took Myrtle Fillmore 7 years. If we don't see results in 2 weeks... we are through with it. That's not how it works. We tell ourselves... *it's not working*. We stop before we have had time to see the inevitable results. This stuff works, but... you're going to have to do it with diligence and persistence. Knowing what to do is not enough. Now that you know how to re-educate every part of yourself... you have to actually do it.

Your voice telling it to yourself has more power over yourself than anyone else.

It worked for Myrtle Fillmore... and it will work for you.

GUILT

It goes without saying that guilt is an unpleasant thing to feel. The weird part is that our Ego is attracted to it, because only the Ego can experience guilt. So while you feel guilty, your Ego is really in control. Let's talk about what differentiates the Ego from the Self. The Ego is the part of yourself that is your personality, while the Super-conscious Mind is that Divine inner part of you. Only your personality can really feel guilt.

Let me tell you something about guilt. If you ever experience it, you will devise a punishment for yourself. Did you know that? You have to have a perception that there is something that you have done to deserve feeling guilty.

Guilt is really a feeling of self-condemnation… one that we experience when we do or even when we think that we do something wrong. But it's impossible to experience feelings of guilt without also anticipating a punishment for ourselves. The real downside to it is that we *will* create the punishment. The guaranteed effects of guilt on each of us are as follows:

First, it makes us feel like we are under attack.
Second, it destroys our self-esteem and our confidence.
It makes us feel depressed, and it denies or destroys our sense of peace.
And finally, it makes us feel unloved.

Whenever you feel guilty for any reason, there is really only one antidote that I know of: Love and self-forgiveness. The thing is… we have to begin by forgiving ourselves, because there's no one else to forgive in the first place. Also don't make it so that you are willing to forgive but not forget. That's not even forgiveness. That's the Ego's way of for- giving… a type of mercy with a loophole in it that pretty much just says, "I will forgive you because I am superior to you, therefore I can sit on my anger and repress it rather than be consciously aware of my desire to hurt you." That is not forgiveness, and if any- thing all it's going to do is further our feeling of separation and guilt.

Freedom and healing which comes from true forgiveness brings us clearly into pure love and unity with all things. The only way you can be truly peaceful and happy is to stay in the present, by doing the best that you can with every moment that is given to you. You know the only Power that you and I have is over the present moment, and we cannot be in the present moment if we have so much guilt behind us in the past. If we are constantly remembering what happened or what we did and didn't do, we are constantly feeling guilt and thus we are powerless at the present moment.

We should be feeling the joy and the love of the world every moment of our days. It all begins with forgiving yourself right now… absolving yourself of all guilt.

Let go of yesterday.
It's in the past and it is gone now.

The only thing… the best thing, in fact… that you can really do about it is just let it go. If you continue feeling guilty about something, it remains in your present and find yourself reliving it over and over and over again.

Work to not make those same mistakes again… but don't dwell on them now that they have come and gone. This isn't about the future, and the past is behind you now. Live for the present. Stay vigilant, and let go of those false perceptions of the world and the people around you. They have their own inner struggles to face anyway.

You have only yourself to forgive so
that you can celebrate life to its fullest.

TO FEAR IS TO SIN

You and I were intended to have everything we need to live a harmonious life. We get so busy with the things we have created that we forget that there is a reason for our being here. Our reason for being here is to find ourselves and to extend love. We need to look within ourselves to deal with whatever issues we may have. The main reason that we don't look within ourselves to deal with our issues is… FEAR.

Fear is our only adversary… personally… nationally… globally. When we are fearful… we face defeat. When you have a fear of lack… a fear of failure… a fear of loss… that fear robs you of your creative power.

Fear is a four-letter word. It ought to be bleeped out every time it is said. God created us, but… we make ourselves, and our circumstances. God created us. What does that mean? It means that humankind was an idea in Universal Mind. You and I take that idea and we make something from it. We are the architects and the builders of our own circum- stances and our destiny. Our lives do not contain any joy or any sadness that was not born in our imagination and then manifested into outward expression. By the power of our thoughts, we create joy or sadness.

Sorrow, sickness, guilt and failure spring from fear and negative thinking. They are always self-imposed. That is the important thing. We think that those things out there that cause us sorrow are beyond our control. But… those things out there… we created them. Usually… we create them from fear. We have this ability to think and to create. If we get on a downward spiral… we begin to fear all things.

My faith is in my Source. When I understand that the Source of my power is greater than anything that I am facing… I do not need to be fearful. God says… *fear not for I am with you. Why are ye fearful, oh ye of little faith?* Fear is nothing more than inverted faith. When we are fearful… we begin to attract to us the very thing that we fear. We are magnetizing it to us.

Remember the story of Daniel and the lion's den? Daniel was undisturbed because he knew that God was stronger than any of those lions. He stayed all night in the lion's den and the lions didn't bother him. He knew that the Power that protected him made those lions harmless. You may say… my faith in God will not make lions harmless. When we connect with the source of our Power… it changes our vibrations. That causes us to become invisible to something of a different vibration. They don't see us as something to go for. That applies to any loin that you have in your life... anything that you fear or worry about.

The greatest fear that we may have may be the fear of loss. Things may be going great. Then… that lion of apprehension comes creeping around. It says… this is too good to be true. It can't last. Then… you get afraid. Your attention goes to that loss… the fear of loss. People have lost what they prized most in life because they worried about losing it. The minute that you spend all of your time worrying about losing something… it's gone. You have attracted to you the thing that will take it away from you.

The only weapon that we can use against that wrong-minded thinking would be our words and our thoughts. God has weapons that we know not of. How do we walk up to those lions that we are fearful of and speak the word? Moses said:

Fear ye not. Stand still and see the salvation of the Lord, which He will show to you this day. For the Egyptians whom you have seen today... ye shall see them again no more... forever. The Lord shall fight for you and ye shall hold your peace.

What a marvelous arrangement. Let God do the fighting for you. Stand still and know that God is God. Infinite Intelligence… God… always knows the way out. Infinite Intelligence knows where the supply is for every demand. We are going to have to trust it. We are going to have to have faith. You can say… I don't know the way out of this… but my Source does, and I'm going to let that work for me.

What am I going to have to do? I'm going to have to get out of the way. I'm to have to stand still and let Infinite Intelligence do it for me. When you run away from a disagreeable situation… the situation runs after you. Don't think that you can run away from your problems. You brought them to you in the first place. They are going to go with you wherever you go. But if you stand still and say… there is a way out of this. I may not be able to see it right now. But… my Source… the Source of my Power... the Source of all Power…knows the way out. Then…be still. Now…what will happen? This grand idea will come to you and you will think… that was a piece of luck. NO. It was not a piece of luck. It is the Infinite Intelligence acting on your behalf. Psalms 27 says:

The Lord is my light and my salvation. Whom shall I fear? The Lord is the strength of my life. Of whom shall I be afraid?

When you understand where your Power is coming from and if you invite it into your life… it will come. But, you must first have faith that it is going to happen. Have faith… fear not. If you get afraid… you have lost your faith. Every healing that Jesus did, He would say… *your faith has made you whole*. He had the Power to do it. But, unless they had the faith to accept it… it didn't happen. How much have we left on the table because we didn't have the faith to accept?

All principles are good. It's only when we fail to use the principles correctly, that we fall short of the mark. That is the original meaning of sin. Jesus would heal and then He would say… go and sin no more. It sounds like He is saying… don't go do bad anymore. NO. That's not what He meant. He meant… don't fall short of the principle… don't engage in wrong-minded thinking….don't be missing the mark.

When the Bible was translated during the Elizabethan era… they needed to come up with a word that meant falling short. There was an archery term that meant falling short of hitting the mark. That word was… SIN. So… sin actually means falling short of hit- ting the mark… falling short of applying the principles… falling short of right-minded thinking.

As you begin to think only good things… no matter what happens to you… then you are continually creating good. Don't fall into fear.

TO FEAR IS TO SIN

Fear is falling short of truth. Truth is always goodness, perfection and wholeness. All of our difficulties are due to the ignorance of truth. When we accept a religious doctrine that teaches us that we are going to have trials and tribulations in this life… we have bought into the doctrine of… a veil of tears. There is no need for us to accept that wrong- minded thinking. It is not the truth. You look around and say… it is so. I can see it. Well… it is so because we have believed that it is so. It all goes back to our error thinking.

The Universe is a Universe of abundance. It only takes a tiny garden plot to feed a large family all winter. For instance… plant one kernel of corn. One kernel produces a stalk. A stalk produces maybe 10 ears. How many kernels are on each ear? See what I mean?

If we look at nature… the Universe… you will see that you and I are meant to live in abundance. The point is… we do live in abundance. If you plant one thought of fear… it's going to produce an abundance of fear. If you plant one thought of happiness… you will have an abundance of happiness. Plant a thought of success… you will reap success. When you plant your seeds… they create an abundance of whatever you have planted. It can go either way on the scale.

Fear makes cowards of us. It makes us do things we should not do. It keeps us afraid to do things that we should do. Whenever we find anything bothering us…we need to apply the Denial/Affirmation process.

Denial:
The fact that I fear… whatever… has no power over me.

Affirmation:
I fear nothing.

So… you are denying the power of fear and you are reinforcing that you have nothing to fear. This will turn things around. If you give into that fear… it will not just manifest… it will manifest in abundance. Abundance is the law of the Universe.

In the Old Testament, Job said… "my fears have come upon me." Of course they did. He manifested them. What are your fears? Whatever they are… face them. What is it that you are afraid of? Don't give it any power. Do the Denial/Affirmation process.

Deny:
Whatever I fear has no power over me.

Affirm:
I AM healthy, strong, young, powerful, loving, harmonious, successful, happy and prosperous.

That just about covers it. There is nothing in this world… out there… that you and I did not create with our thoughts. So… if we created it with our thoughts… we can un-create it with our thoughts.

FDR said:
"We have nothing to fear but fear, itself."

That's the truth. You can change anything. There is nothing in this world that cannot be changed with the changing of your thinking. If you are afraid of something… you have to deny the fear, and affirm the truth.

The truth is:
I have nothing to fear.
God is my source.
Nothing is powerful enough to stand in front of God.

CELEBRATING LIFE

We need to take time to celebrate. An attitude of celebration would help our lives immensely. We need to wake up and celebrate life. When you are celebrating… you are in a fantastic mood. Mood has everything to do with what is going to happen next.

What happens does not create your mood. Your mood creates what happens. Creating the mood for the expectation is actually more fun than the realization of the expectation. As you begin to *enjoy* your life, day by day, and *celebrate* that life, day by day, the *rewards* for living life, day by day, will *come* to us.

There is a law called the law of reversal. We say that we are happy because we have achieved our goal. However… the process works equally well in the reverse direction. We can achieve or goal because we have assumed the happy feeling of the expectation fulfilled. How would you feel if the thing you wanted most in life were yours… right now? Can you imagine how you would feel?

Moods are not only the result of conditions… they are the causes of those conditions. You and I look around to see if we can have any indicators of an outcome, and that constitutes what our mood is going to be. Instead… we should assume the mood that if all the indicators were… GO…. GO… FABULOUS. Now… watch the indicators reflect the desired outcome.

An idea produces nothing and does nothing. It only acts when it is fully felt. You get an idea about something and then your feeling about that idea indicates how it is going to turn out. We all get ideas all the time. But… along with that idea comes… I could do that… that would be fun… that would be easy… or… I could never do that… or… I'm not good enough to do that. Whatever it is that we attach to that idea… determines how it is going to turn out.

If you have an idea and you think… NO… I don't know how to do that… or… NO… that wouldn't work for me… that will not bring success if that is your attachment to the idea. What we need to learn to do is to capture the feeling of… isn't that wonderful. What would it feel like if you said that? What is the feeling of…something wonderful is happening to me?

Isn't it w o n d e f u l?
WOW!
Say it aloud right now.
Isn't it w o n d e r f u l?

You may be waiting for me to say… what's wonderful? I'm not going to say. It doesn't matter. What we have to do is get that attitude about life. We have to get that feeling that something wonderful is happening to me….RIGHT NOW! It's the celebration. Can you go to sleep every night saying? Isn't it wonderful… something wonderful is happening to me now.

When we do this with a feeling of joy for everyone… we don't have to have a thought of how will this happen? It's just a feeling of joy… Peace on earth and goodwill to all. We are all happy… isn't it wonderful? The mood of an expectation fulfilled is really the high tide that can lift you up and easily move you up from where you are stuck… where you are stranded. It can move you to another place. The high tide that can pick you up and move you.

This is not just talking in the wind. This is how you and I can live in this world and live a beautiful life. Whatever mood it is that we have at all times is going to be what hap- pens to us. If achieving an expectation establishes a certain mood… then the law of reversal says… if you achieve that mood… then the expectation will be established. We live in a world of order… a world of balance. This is orderly. You ask… how can a mood bring about an expectation? Well… that's METAPHYSICS. That gets way above the law of the brain. That is the law of the mind… the Mind of God.

Our moods affirm what will come to pass. You find whatever you are looking for. If you are looking for things not to go well… you find that things don't go well. If you are looking for the success… you will find success. It is different with each individual. The circumstances can be identical. One person sees success and another person sees failure. One person lives their success and the other person lives their failure.

This is a story about warts. It is a story of attitude, expectation and outcome. This fellow told his son who had some wart on his knees… I'll buy those warts from you. But… if I buy them… you can't have them anymore. They decided on ten cents a wart. They counted the warts. The father said… if I give you this money… the warts are mine… you can't have them anymore. The boy agreed. So… he sold his dad the warts. Within 3 weeks… every wart was gone. The boy was not even surprised. That is what he expected. He said… I sold them to dad. He had the expectation that they were gone. So… they left.

Our attitudes… our moods… our expectations… are so powerful. We don't give them credit. We say… what does it matter that I'm in a bad mood? Well… it matters. It matters what is going to happen in your life. If you can't be in a good mood 100% of the time… give it your best shot. It is better to be happy 95% of the time than to be happy 50% of the time.

Life is so perfect. As we begin to see it that way…it begins to manifest that way. From this point on…let's wake up every morning and say:

THANK YOU, GOD, FOR THIS WONDERFUL LIFE. ISN'T IT WONDERFUL!

THAT IS THE ART OF CELEBRATING LIFE

PERSONAL ASSESSMENT

The left hand side of the worksheets refers to WRONG-MINDED THINKING responses. The right hand side refers to the alternative RIGHT-MINDED THINKING response.

Score yourself at least once a week and make your entries in pencil since the score can change each time you make an entry.

Low scores are a red flag that you are coming from WRONG-MINDED THINKING in your daily transactions … that you may be engaging in Crossed Transactions … that you may be playing harmful EGO games.

Practicing Self-Hypnosis regularly will allow you to reinforce your Sub-Conscious Mind with RIGHT-MINDED THINKING suggestions, giving automatic RIGHT-MINDED guidance to your Conscious Mind

You are entitled to be the successful person you were created to be.

It is your birthright.

CONGRATULATIONS!

PERSONAL ASSESSMENT

SCORE	WRONG-MINDED THINKING 0<5	RIGHT-MINDED THINKING 6>10
	Resentful	Pleased for others
	Dishonest	Honest
	Self-pity	Self-confidence
	Jealous	Happy for others
	Critical	Supportive
	Fearful	Fearless
	Anxiety	Confidence
	Dread	Joyful anticipation
	Worry	Confident
	Uncertainty…chance	Goal-setting
	Apprehension	Concern
	Anger	Tolerance
	False pride	Pride
	Vindictive…vengful	Helpful
	Intolerance	Forgiveness
	Impatient	Patient
	Perpetuate problems	Solve problems
	Gossip	Do not spread rumors
	Belittles	Praises
	Shouts	Speaks calmly
	Scorn	Praises
	Wrath	Tolerance
	Conceit…self-centered	Self-confidence
	Vain	Well-groomed
	Mentally lazy	Studious
	Excess	Moderation
	Neglectful	Caring
	Selfish	Considerate
	Short-sighted	Visionary
	Boastful	Humble
	Cheats	Faithful
	Takes for granted	Appreciative
	Blames others	Admits errors
	Makes excuses	Makes amends
	Hypocritical	Straight-forward…honest
	Depressed	Happy…cheerfful
	Frowns	Smiles
	Dictatorial	Participative
	Over-powering	Participative
	Unwise	Wise
	Lazy…slothful	Diligent
	Fruitless Ambition	Ambition

PERSONAL ASSESSMENT

SCORE	WRONG-MINDED THINKING 0<5	RIGHT-MINDED THINKING 6>10
	Manipulative	Honest
	Naïve…ignorant	Informed
	Defensive	Confident
	Offensive	Confident
	Abusive	Caring
	Cynical	Cheery
	Self-rightous	Honest
	Cowardly	Brave
	Flagrant	Discreet
	Appart from God	Close to God
	Neglects prayer	Prays regularly
	Neglects meditaion	Meditates regularly
	Unhealthy habits	Healthy habits
	Questions…analyzes	Accepts
	Perception	Knowledge
	Illusion	Reality
	Separation	Atonement
	Attack	Forgiveness
	My will	God's Will
	Grandiosity	Grandeur
	Projection	Extension
	Crusifixion	Resurrection
	Physical	Spiritual
	Wrath of God	Love of God
	Sin	Correction
	Fear	Love
	Guilt	Forgiveness
	Attack	Love
	Anger	Love
	Hate	Love

APPENDIX

What You See Is What Will Be

By Jim Johnson ©1987

TO ACHIEVE YOUR POTENTIAL... REMEMBER YOUR A B C'S

Asking **HOLY SPRIIT** for guidance from A to Z

Avoid negative sources…people…places…things…habits.
Believe in yourself.
Consider things from every angle
Don't give up…and don't give in.
Enjoy life today…yesterday is gone…tomorrow may never come.
Family and friends are hidden treasures…seek them…enjoy their riches.
Give more than you planned to give.
Hand out Love.
Ignore those who try to discourage you.
Just do it!
Keep on trying no matter how hard it seems…it will get easier.
Love yourself first and most.
Make it happen!
Never lie…cheat…steal. Always strike a fair deal.
Open your eyes and see the truth.
Perfect practice makes perfect.
Quitters never win…winners never quit.
Read, study and learn about everything important in your life.
Stop procrastinating
Take control of your own destiny.
Understand yourself to better understand others.
Visualize it.
Want it more than anything.
X-celerate your efforts
You are a unique creation of God…nothing can replace you.
Zero in on your target…and go for it.

The Bank of the Universe is now open!

It has *unlimited abundance*, available to you right now!

Actually it has never NOT been open,
but only a few throughout the history of mankind knew of the unlimited abundance
that was theirs for the asking.

You must believe that you can receive it,
so take small steps with the amounts,
if that feels more believable to you.

Place the check in a prominent position
where you will see it every day!

Every time you look at the check,
STOP!!! BELIEVE and FEEL
that you have the money
NOW!

The *Universe* inspires people, circumstances and events, to deliver the amount to you, but don't ever be mistaken into believing it came *from* them.

It is always the *Universe*, who moves *through* people, circumstances and events, to deliver it to you.

If YOU don't cancel your check, *The Bank of the Universe* must deliver the money to you!

Any thoughts, words, or actions of "lack", or "not enough"... are the only things that cancel your check.

Here's the great thing though... if you are thinking, acting or speaking words that could cancel your check, the *Universe* immediately sends you an alert! The alert is instantaneously transmitted direct to you, as bad feelings!!! The moment you receive the alert, change your thinking immediately!

By the way, it is not your job to work out HOW the *Universe* will bring it to you, so hands off telling the *Universe* what to do. Just ask, believe you have received it, and you WILL receive.

Here is the check.
Fill in your name and the amount you wish to receive.

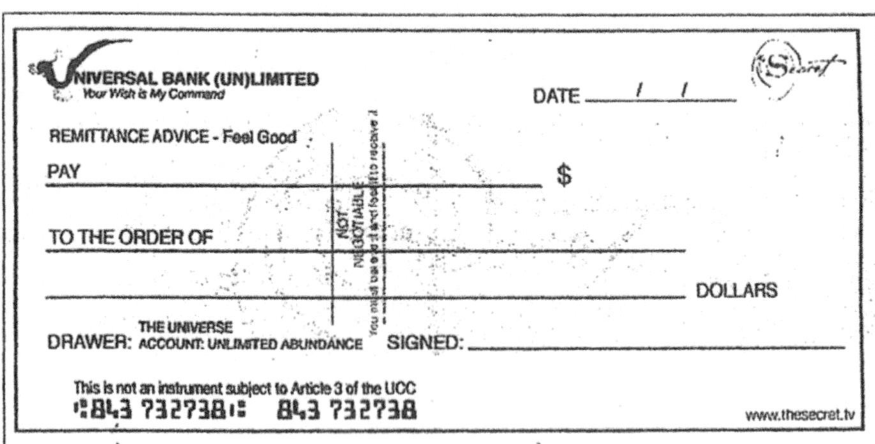

PUBLICATIONS
BY
JIM JOHNSON

BOOKS

CELEBRATING LIFE
WELCOME TO THE STATE OF JOY
SUCCESS THROUGH SELF-HYPNOSIS

CD'S

HYPNODYNAMIX
THE ALPHA STATE OF CONSCIOUSNESS

BOOKS ARE AVAILABLE FROM:
www.dogearpublishing.net

ALL PUBLICATIONS ARE AVAILABLE FROM:
www.amazon.com

Jim's Books and ebooks
are available on Amazon.com

Made in the USA
Monee, IL
20 October 2026

66035285R00085